CIVIL WAR
RICHMOND

CIVIL WAR RICHMOND

The Last Citadel

JACK TRAMMELL & GUY TERRELL

FOREWORD BY ED AYERS

THE
History
PRESS

Published by The History Press
Charleston, SC
www.historypress.com

Cover image: Currier & Ives print, Metropolitan Museum.

First published 2021

Manufactured in the United States

ISBN 9781467145893

Library of Congress Control Number: 2020951658

Notice: The information in this book is true and complete to the best of our knowledge. It is offered without guarantee on the part of the authors or The History Press. The authors and The History Press disclaim all liability in connection with the use of this book.

CONTENTS

CONTENTS

FOREWORD

Richmond stood on the major fault lines of the United States. In 1860, the city was national and southern, industrial and agrarian, African American and immigrant, defining itself by the past and yet thoroughly modern. Richmond became the capital of the Confederacy precisely because it occupied the edge of the would-be nation, boasting extensive railroad connections and the Tredegar Iron Works while also shipping thousands of people every year from the exhausted farms and plantations of Virginia to the raw new plantations of the southern frontier.

In months-long sessions at the capitol, delegates from across the Commonwealth voted over and over again not to secede, despite the lobbying of Confederate agents, and then abruptly changed course when President Lincoln called on Virginia to supply troops to help put down the rebellion in South Carolina. Delegates opposed to secession warned what would happen if Virginia joined the revolt against the United States: it would become the battleground of the nation. Its economy would be devastated, its cities burned, its families shattered and its slave system destroyed.

All those things came to pass. Richmond immediately found itself engulfed by the war. From the first battles, the bodies of young men groaned into the city on the railroads that had promised prosperity only months before, with shattered lives filling stores and houses suddenly made into hospitals. Massive armies and navies converged on the Confederate capital, threatening from every direction, its defenders as well as its attackers consuming food that could have sustained civilians. Tens of thousands of people flooded into the small city, overwhelming its capacity to absorb them. People held in slavery watched, looking for opportunity to escape and hoping for signs that their bondage would end.

Jack Trammel and Guy Terrell know this city and this story well. They evoke the chaos of the Confederate years, showing how Richmond's story embodied that of the rebellion with which it would be forever identified. Using powerful photographs and the latest research, they portray a city with all its contradictions exposed. Anyone who would understand Richmond today must understand Civil War Richmond, and in this book they will find windows into that world.

—EDWARD L. AYERS

INTRODUCTION

Any good history begins in strangeness. The past should not be comfortable. The past should not be a familiar echo of the present, for if it is familiar why revisit it? The past should be so strange that you wonder how you and people you know and love could come from such a time.
—Richard White, historian of the American West

For us and other historians, the Confederate capital of Richmond has been as hard to subdue intellectually as it was militarily for a host of Lincoln's generals and their Union troops. What Richmond was like between 1861 and 1865 becomes clearer with the publication of every new study. Richmond as the Confederate capital existed on the fault line between a society based on the enslavement of African Americans and a society where more and more citizens found slavery to be unacceptable in a growing industrial nation based on the premise of freedom equally available to all. Richmond today still reflects physically the remnants of what is known as the Lost Cause—the idea that the Civil War was a just and heroic struggle for a way of life and for states' rights. The current debate over the removal of monuments dedicated to Confederate "heroes" on Monument Avenue reflects even today the legacy of the defeat.

We believe that citizens of Richmond rallied almost universally, at first, to the Southern ideology of the right to secede from the Union and believed that slavery was morally defensible. Those opposed to this view existed, but their ideals were suppressed on the streets of Richmond at the time Lincoln was elected in 1860. It is nearly impossible to know the mind of any individual. For example, General Winfield Scott, whose wife was from Richmond and owned a farm at the edge of the city (now known as the commercial area Scott's Addition), stayed in the Union army and devised the "Anaconda" blockade of the South. Robert E. Lee, also an officer in the U.S. Army, resigned his post to stay with his home state and valiantly defended the Confederacy.

Primo Levi, a Holocaust survivor and writer, stated that we lack the ability to accurately perceive the experiences of others. We cannot fully understand what made so many Confederate generals, officers, political leaders and those with no economic interest in maintaining slavery ultimately fight for and advance the Confederate cause. But they devoted all of their efforts to defeat the Union armies all over the South.

Richmond in 1861 was a medium-size U.S. city situated below the Mason-Dixon line with strong Mid-Atlantic and southern commercial and cultural ties. It was the twenty-fifth-largest city in 1860; today, in the most recent census, it ranks ninety-eighth. It was in many ways a quintessentially American city—rapidly industrializing, establishing financial infrastructure and connecting to other places around the globe. It came to represent the darker side of the American experience as the key center for the slave trade and the capital of a bitter armed rebellion intended to preserve it.

The city was, at times, almost an extension of the battlefield, surrounded by armed encampment, thronged with wounded and with prisoners, infused with the sights and smells and sounds of death.
—*Virginia Sharff, from* Introduction to Richmond during the War *by Sallie Brock Putnam*

Our book reflects all aspects of the city but particularly aims to capture the human face of the wartime experience. Social historians endeavor to move beyond simply names and dates. Instead, we want to show the lived emotions and real human encounters that made up part of the unpredictable fabric of what we call history but at the time created frightening uncertainty for those experiencing it.

Such an amazing story cannot be covered adequately in a few hundred pages or less. It forces us to distill the key elements and consider what the truly significant and meaningful things were across the population spectrum. We hope that you'll read more about Richmond during the Civil War after you read this book, as inevitably some important events and social trends get left out.

—Jack Trammell
Spring 2020

PART I

RICHMOND BEFORE 1861

Chapter 1

ANTEBELLUM RICHMOND

The city of Richmond in 1860 was a snapshot of the amazing American success story—modern and industrializing, with public transportation, banks, city water and gas, theaters and colleges, plus quiet and prosperous neighborhoods. A visitor to Richmond in 1860 from other parts of North America would have seen very little that was unfamiliar or surprising. The hustle and bustle of new businesses like photography were booming as people from near and far came to the myriad gallery shops to have their image rendered in vivid realism. Circuses routinely performed here. Richmond in 1860 had a history old enough to include famous heroes and founders, such as George Washington, whose famous equestrian statue by Thomas Crawford still stands beside the capitol building designed by Thomas Jefferson. It took pride in St. John's Episcopal Church, where Patrick Henry delivered his "Give me liberty or give me death!" speech that helped set the American Revolution in motion. The faithful still worship there. Also, the home of Supreme Court chief justice John Marshall, who shaped many of the nation's early laws, still stands today open to the public. While it was in many ways an ordinary city for its time and place, it contained significant ties to the founding of our nation. Events shortly to unfold would forever make it an extraordinary and unforgettable city.

To this point, what made Richmond famous were events, people and ideas that were well known to Virginia schoolchildren: explorer John Smith sailing up the James River in 1607 to first scout the seven hills; William Mayo, friend of Willian Byrd II, finishing his initial survey of Richmond in 1737; the capital of Virginia moving from Williamsburg to Richmond in 1780, placing it farther away from the British and closer to interior economic expansion; British troops under traitor Benedict Arnold burning the city on January 5, 1781, just months before the surrender of Lord Cornwallis in Yorktown; and a great fire burning the Richmond Theatre in 1811, killing seventy-two people. The war years, however, would rewrite all of that history and supplant it with something so dramatic that the scars and memories remain with the city permanently.

The descriptions of the city on the eve of the war speak for themselves, as a contemporary author captured well:

> *A century and a half later, we can still sample Pizzini's menu from his long-vanished Confectionery shop on Broad Street and laugh over the public's abuse heaped upon an ungainly goose statue at Capitol Square. We can still gasp at the attempt to launch a giant balloon carrying a mounted horse at Ashland and relish the staggering number of foul names that Governor Wise could be called in one short editorial by the* Richmond *Whig. Whether it be graffiti in a park bathroom, enduring someone smoking in public, eating Indian "popped" corn at amusements, or the mighty being caught with their hand in the cookie jar, through these scenes and recollections we remain connected to a bygone world whose people remain surprisingly familiar.*[1]

It would be a great disservice to over-romanticize the setting too much, but for the period prior to the war, Richmond was as cosmopolitan and progressive as anywhere else, a bustling center of human activity and as "American" as any other city in almost all ways (excepting the evil of slavery, which was present in many but not all American cities; there were even slaves in prewar Pittsburgh). Celebrated British author Charles Dickens visited Richmond in 1842 and recorded his thoughts about a city that would be analogous in 1860:

> *The next day, and the next, we rode and walked about the town, which is delightfully situated on eight hills, overhanging the James River; a sparkling stream, studded here and there with bright islands, or brawling over broken rocks. Although it was yet but the middle of March, the weather in this southern temperature was extremely warm; the peach-trees and magnolias were in full bloom* [he got that wrong—magnolias bloom in June]*; and the trees were green. In a low ground among the hills, is a valley known*

as "Bloody Run," from a terrible conflict with the Indians which once occurred there. It is a good place for such a struggle, and, like every other spot I saw associated with any legend of that wild people now so rapidly fading from the earth, interested me very much.

Dickens was rather outspoken in his reaction to and critique of American race-based slavery, especially so when around the business aspects of it in Richmond. He also caught a glimpse of the burgeoning tobacco industry in action:

I saw in this place the whole process of picking, rolling, pressing, drying, packing in casks, and branding. All the tobacco thus dealt with, was in course of manufacture for chewing; and one would have supposed there was enough in that one storehouse to have filled even the comprehensive jaws of America. In this form, the weed looks like the oil-cake on which we fatten cattle; and even without reference to its consequences, is sufficiently uninviting.

When he asked to visit with the enslaved employees on their lunch break, he was rebuffed. Many Richmonders were suspicious, defensive and even paranoid when it came to outsider curiosity about the "peculiar institution." During the war, the Richmond attitude about race would cycle through many additional complications, particularly as the war forced citizens to acquiesce to giving free and enslaved African Americans more independence to support the war effort. Dickens, at the time, was not impressed:

To those who are happily unaccustomed to them, the countenances in the streets and labouring-places, too, are shocking. All men who know that there are laws against instructing slaves, of which the pains and penalties greatly exceed in their amount the fines imposed on those who maim and torture them, must be prepared to find their faces very low in the scale of intellectual expression. But the darkness—not of skin, but mind—which meets the stranger's eye at every turn; the brutalizing and blotting out of all fairer characters traced by Nature's hand; immeasurably outdo his worst belief.

Southerners who visited Richmond and were perhaps more accepting of the racial hierarchy than others found other things to admire about the city. It was situated on dramatic rapids in the river and had an international port and rich farmland spread out on seven bucolic hills.

Richmond was the second home of iconic American author Edgar Allan Poe. Born in Boston in 1809, tragedy stalked the early part of his life. His parents were actors and performers. While in Richmond playing at the Richmond Theatre, his mother took ill and died shortly thereafter, leaving Poe (almost three years old) and his infant sister instant orphans. The theater tragically burned down a few days later, killing many prominent Virginians, including the governor.

Poe was adopted by the Allan family in Richmond, and when the Monumental Church was built on top of the theater ruins in memory of the fire, the Allan family reserved pew number eighty to attend services. Although Poe moved away in his college years, he returned in 1835 to be editor of the *Southern Literary Messenger*. His reputation would permanently be associated with Richmond, and by the time of the Civil War, most of the homes and businesses he had frequented were still extant.

Richmond in 1860 was literate, prosperous, cultured, international and thriving. Several foreign cities had consulates here due to the tobacco trade. The U.S. Census of 1860 counted 1,623 Germans in Richmond, or more than 4 percent of the population; along with other foreigners, they totaled 13 percent. Little did anyone expect that the city would soon experience something terrible that no other American city ever had gone through before.

Chapter 2

RICHMOND, 1840–1860

C ommerce has always suited Richmond due to its pivotal geographic location. Originally, an American Indian village stood on the hills above the James River at the Fall Line, and the river enabled easy access to the Chesapeake Bay and the Atlantic Ocean. Native trails running up and down the coast (along what is now Interstate 95 and Interstate 64) provided access by horse, by wagon and by foot. Other major trails led west to the Appalachian Mountains and Shenandoah Valley, with some down into Southside Virginia and the Carolinas. Richmond was a natural connecting point with abundant game, timber and fresh water.

The location was originally settled by Algonquin natives; Europeans moved into the region in the early to mid-seventeenth century. They brought enslaved and indentured servants with them. From that time forward, imported slave labor became the primary pillar supporting the frontier and farming economy that led to the rapidly accelerating commercialization of the city. The tobacco industry at the time was the raison d'être for slavery, but later, in Richmond, the slave trade itself would quickly become a much larger industry than tobacco. Over time, the first homes and small businesses began to coalesce in the area that would be incorporated as the town of Richmond in 1742.

The impact of slavery and the slave trade on Richmond's (and soon the nation's) economy was profound. The social and cultural impact is sometimes much harder to quantify but was just as profound. Richmond's Civil War

Slave Memorial Marker, along Fifteenth Street. *Photo by Derek Kannemeyer.*

story is irrevocably tied to the story of the slave trade, as well as the legal, legislative, commercial and religious contexts that began to define and then to codify the elements that would comprise a slavocracy.

By the Civil War, Richmond attitudes about slavery were curiously separate from attitudes about the business itself and people conducting the human chattel transactions. Slave traders and businesses directly involved in the slave trade operated under a social stigma so powerful that men often used aliases or false names when engaging in transactions. Such brokers and traders were sometimes referred to politely as "seconds," meaning they were standing in for someone else, representing the interests of someone much wealthier and with social standing that shouldn't be needlessly risked. Legislators and bureaucrats working around Capitol Square, the heart of the city, only a few blocks away from the "Wall Street" of the Richmond slave trade (literally a street named Wall Street where many of the slave houses or agents were located between Fifteenth and Sixteenth Streets), avoided walking through or being seen in the neighborhood.

The subtle aspects of the business of slavery intersected with the wider complexities of Richmond attitudes about the institution of slavery and, where in conflict, were dominated by economics. Attitudes about slavery, far from monolithic as even some contemporary historians would have readers believe, actually varied widely. There were outright abolitionists, including members of religious communities like Quakers, plus "colonizers"—those who wished to see slaves freed and then sent to Africa to begin again as an independent community. Others believed that manumission, buying slaves and setting them free, would eventually weaken the system enough to cause it to wither away on its own. They sometimes liberated one person at a time as their personal funds permitted. Agnostics, who privately found slavery distasteful and perhaps felt it left a negative mark on polite society, often appeared to have no purely moral objection to it and wouldn't speak out against it. Capitalists saw it purely as a cash bonanza similar to bull stock markets that could be ridden to rapid wealth if timed right. Some small farmers and the less affluent envisioned slavery as a means to gain status and create generational wealth. Other adamant defenders of the institution argued embryonic eugenics. They referenced the Bible and any other argument they could articulate to justify the inferiority of the African-American race and the supposed benevolence of the chattel system.

The primary driving force for slavery in the antebellum era generally consisted of the planter class across the Deep South. Cotton production required more slaves to maintain the level of output and therefore raised the overall level of slave sales. But as slaves aged and couldn't work as hard, younger slaves were needed, plus deaths required replacements. Additionally, other profitable crops such as sugarcane, rice and tobacco were labor-intensive.

Richmonders and other entrepreneurs saw the slave trade as a form of currency, like a pre-modern stock market exchange. Richmond would soon be the center of a capitalist, speculative, highly specialized race-based system never seen before in human history, one that reached its zenith in the Civil War.

KING COTTON

Cotton, long sought as the primary component for fabric, could only be produced in small quantities because the cotton was so difficult to separate from the seed (the boll). By chance, Catharine Greene, widow of Revolutionary War hero Nathanael Greene, noticed the mechanical aptitude of a young tutor, Eli Whitney, visiting overseer Phineas Miller at her plantation, Mulberry Hill, in coastal Georgia. They told Whitney about the difficulty of separating the cotton from the seed inside bolls. Within ten days in the spring of 1793, he had created the cotton gin (short for "engine"). Now a single person using the device could separate fifty times as much cotton as he might have done by hand. Whitney was a graduate of Yale University. Wittingly or not, everyone was complicit in the ascendency of slavery.

With this invention, cotton production soared for the next fifty years, creating a planter class whose wealth consisted of slaves and land. Cotton production at the end of the War of 1812 was estimated to be 150,000 bales. By 1860, however, annual production consisted of 4 million bales. In 1857, cotton rose to $0.15 per pound, with a bale containing five hundred pounds. A bale sold for $75.00, and the total value of 4 million bales was hence $300 million—a phenomenal sum in 1860. Cotton was the largest commodity in the nation and the nation's top export. Not only did textile mills in states like Massachusetts buy it, but much of the production was also exported to Britain and France.

To produce this abundance, planters devoted more and more acreage to cotton between 1810 and 1860. Farmers in those days were not particularly good stewards of the land. Land in the eastern states along the Atlantic wore out. Slave owners there had less need for slaves and began to sell their slaves on the Richmond slave market. Those slaves mainly ended up on plantations farther west. While about a quarter of all farmers owned some slaves, every farmer aspired to become a slave owner. The mindset of the South was to maintain slavery and perhaps personally profit from it. The true planter class, those who owned one hundred slaves or more, was small—roughly two thousand families. They were today's 1 percenters. Their wealth consisted of the value of their slaves and their land. They exerted significant influence because of their wealth and status within their communities. This was the backdrop of the South prior to the Civil War.

The slave trade existed as a by-product of the expansion of cotton farming across the Deep South (the first Confederate States). The realities of the South's agricultural economy drove the desire to defend slavery among citizen-farmers, churches, local governments, courts, state legislatures and, ultimately, the laws of the nation from its founding until 1860. Most southerners could not imagine any other way they could thrive or even live. It was all they had ever known—all they wanted to know.

OPPONENTS OF SLAVERY

The South was not a monolithic culture, and there were a surprising number of individuals and groups that actively opposed the institution of slavery, often at great risk to themselves. The Quaker community in Richmond was adamantly antislavery. It worked secretly to undermine the slave trade. Although the underground nature of its activity means that records are sometimes hard to find, the Confederate government documented its activities. A special part of the Castle Thunder hospital/prison was reserved for domestic agitators, including anyone who might interfere with or protest the slave trade and the associated network of banks, merchants, shippers, agents and owners. When Sheridan burned the Valley of Virginia in 1864, Mennonites and others who were Unionists were driven from their homes as well. Sheridan acknowledged their loyalty but still said they supported the Confederacy by producing wheat and other products that were used by the army.

Quakers, regardless of region, had always been against the institution of slavery (as had some other churches and denominations). Patrick Henry had worked with Quakers in and around Richmond, as well as others during the Revolutionary period, to explore ways to end slavery. They were unsuccessful.

Ultimately, the economic power of slavery overpowered any isolated resistance in the South, and Richmond became the epicenter of a multimillion-dollar internal trade that sent more than 500,000 humans south in bondage. Slaves had their own forms of resistance—slowing work, feigning illness, breaking tools and so on—but their opportunities were increasingly limited by statute and culture, as well as the omnipresent threat of violence or separation.

Resistance to the slave system in mainstream Richmond culture was subject to extreme social pressure and sometimes legal consequences or even outright violence. White Southern dissenters or Unionists were sometimes confined in slave jails rather than normal jails when they interfered with slave trade business. The message was intentional. Charles Miller, for example, was held at Castle Godwin:

> It is claimed by those who ought to know, that Miller is a "red-hot abolitionist." Perhaps his red republican socialistic ideas may incline him that way. At any rate, it would appear that he does not have a very good idea of his duties as a citizen of this great and desireable [sic] Confederacy.[2]

Others, such as the infamous Elizabeth Van Lew, were either more subtle or able to work more deftly behind the scenes. Enterprising family members could surreptitiously have family slaves assigned work on the outer fortifications, for example, where it was known that slaves could escape to Union lines with more ease. The risks were high, and unfortunately few Richmonders choose to challenge the system or risk their own safety to help free enslaved African Americans.

The cruelties of slavery are not to be dismissed in any way by the wide variety of statuses and privileges (or lack thereof) that both free African Americans and those in bondage experienced during the war years. Richmond, like slavery itself, was a culture in dizzying transition in 1861. It is a sober reminder to see the numerous accounts of slave punishments and executions for violating norms and laws that brought the wrong kind of attention. A slave named Richard, in a case that illustrates many others, was executed in 1863 in the Henrico Jail Yard at the Courthouse, according to the April 5, 1863 *Dispatch*, for attacking his male overseer (ironically, the woman from New York who owned him was leasing him in Virginia—apparently it was legal to own slaves in Virginia and still live in a slave-free state):

> *When the near approach of death unnerved him…he made a full and free confession to Rev. Mr. Christian, of Union Station, his spiritual attendant. The above execution was known to but few at the time of its occurrence. A dozen persons were present—not more. The culprit died easy, and on the same gallows on which Louis Napoleon was executed some months since.*

In the final analysis, the Confederacy couldn't have entered into a meaningful bid for independence without the tangible value of slave labor and the more esoteric but equally important capitalized asset they represented for purposes of credit, banking and national economic budgeting. During the war, Richmond's importance as the primary market (New Orleans fell early in the war) meant that secondary and tertiary markets tended to become even more closely connected to Richmond.

RICHMOND BEFORE 1861

IMPORTANCE OF THE
AFRICAN-AMERICAN COMMUNITY TO RICHMOND

African Americans, both free and in bondage, formed a sizable portion of the population in Richmond, slightly greater than one-third by 1861, and contributed in many important ways to the character and success of the city:

> The Heslip and Ruffin families were active as African American leaders since the time of Nancy and George W. Ruffin, antebellum free Blacks from Virginia. Members of the families were active in the areas of politics, publishing and editing, and law. Nancy Ruffin (1816–1874) and George W. Ruffin (1800–1863) were free Blacks during the antebellum era residing in Richmond, Virginia. George W. worked as a barber, and both he and Nancy valued education and hired a tutor to teach their children English literature, Latin and the classics. Following the prohibition by the Virginia legislature against African Americans learning to read, Nancy moved to Boston in 1853 along with their eight children, while George W remained in Virginia and sent funds for the family's support. Following the move to Boston, Nancy sold fish and fruit sent by family in the South.[3]

The African-American community held its own prior to and during the Civil War. While it cannot be said to have flourished, its institutions and churches grasped the importance of nurturing families and individuals. Ignoring the many laws and restrictions was the most effective approach. If the Public Guard, local law enforcement and Confederate security forces are watching at the walls, they cannot enforce all the laws as well as prepare and maintain fortifications. Law enforcement had to monitor dissenters, soldiers on leave, thousands of new residents and slaves brought to Richmond to be hired out as workers across all the burgeoning war industries needing workers or to replace those enlisted in the army. The 1860 census recorded 11,739 slaves living in Richmond—almost one-third of the city's population. We do not know how many African Americans were in Richmond between 1861 and 1865 because slaves came to Richmond from many sources. Some slaves accompanied soldiers who enlisted, and others fled with their owners from areas occupied by Union troops. Richmond during the war was a metropolis constantly in flux, and this provided new options for African Americans.

Churches were an acceptable institution to the white power structure as a place where African Americans could gather. Churches with African-American members by law had to have white ministers. Before the war,

25

there were four Baptist churches and one Methodist church. The four Baptist churches had about 4,600 members—over one-third of the city's African-American population. The ministers followed a formulaic ministry and doctrine. They preached white supremacy and obedience by members. Churches also had deacons and other lay leaders. This was one of the few acceptable arenas where African-American men and women could express their leadership abilities. They organized weddings and funerals and other social activities that helped bind people together. It was also good practice that served the African-American community well in the next one hundred years of the battles for civil rights. There were other fraternal organizations primarily for "the interment of the dead." Richmond had a series of African-American cemeteries for both slave and freed since about 1800. Some of those after the Civil War are marked and under restoration today.

Individuals resisted white supremacy by learning to read. Not an easy thing to achieve since it was prohibited as well. But they heard Bible verses read in church and had access to Bibles. Thomas Johnson taught himself to read. By his mid-twenties, he could make sense of newspapers. A slave named Fields Cook earned money for himself and his owner during the first half of the nineteenth century as a barber and a "leech doctor." He was able to purchase his freedom and that of his wife and child. He acquired real estate. His master may have taught him to read and write to manage his business. By 1860, Cook and seventy other free African Americans owned property totaling nearly $185,000. Members contributed generously to the only institution where they were truly free. African-American churches reflected finer furnishings and appointments than most possessed at home. This was a way not only to glorify God but also to demonstrate a status equal with white society. Churches were the first steppingstone to wider freedom even before the Civil War.

African Americans became entrepreneurs, especially those who were freed even before the Civil War. During the war, African-American women offered food and snacks at the railway stations. Gambling, prostitution and saloons opened other opportunities to the community during the war. The rising prosperity of many African Americans did not go unnoticed by the courts or by newspapers, which commented on violations of laws against African Americans riding in hacks or carriages. As the war progressed and violations of ordinances mounted, law enforcement conducted more arrests, and the courts handed down harsher punishments. Stephen Ash noted that "a free black cookshop proprietor named William Ferguson was arrested in 1864 for 'keeping a disorderly house,' that being his shop, where, it was alleged, 'white men and negroes sit at the same table and devour delicacies.'"

COMPILATION OF STORIES INTO ONE PASTICHE

In 1860, Silas Washington was a twenty-two-year-old African-American slave, born on a medium-size plantation near Staunton in Augusta County, Virginia. Silas did a variety of jobs on the plantation where he lived with his mother and extended family, which was really a large farm compared to the true one-crop Tidewater plantations farther eastward and southward. These included everything from running a plow and other implements behind oxen to cutting and hauling firewood and everything else in between. In fact, Silas learned some basic blacksmithing from another slave on the farm and also taught himself how to make shoes from leather combined with other local products.

In early 1861, a rumor spread among the several dozen farm slaves that someone had tried to run away and been caught. A quick count showed that everyone known on the farm was accounted for. Nonetheless, the farm owner, William Franklin, showed up shortly thereafter with an African-American man in shackles and several other white strangers and demanded that everyone show up in the central yard between the main house and outbuildings. Silas and the others were forced to watch a terrible flogging of a man from nearby Staunton who had failed in his escape attempt. The message was clear.

In the summer of 1861, William Franklin unexpectedly told Silas that he was being sold to the local Lutheran congregation to which Franklin belonged. Franklin assured him that this was much more humane than being "sold South" or being sent to the teeming markets in Richmond. In fact, Franklin claimed that his Lutheran faith was against the general principles of slavery but that the law and economy of the times would not tolerate its abolition. The church would rent him out to generate revenue to support the church (i.e., pay its pastor; repair the building; fund mission work and so on), so in a strange way, Franklin felt he was doing right by both Silas and the church. It was also likely that Silas would continue to work in the immediate area, and since he had a reputation as a "problem-free" slave, he would also likely be able to visit with his mother and others he knew on a regular basis without much difficulty. At first, Franklin's words seemed mostly true. Silas painted the entire church, made shoes in nearby Verona and was allowed to keep a small portion of the proceeds for himself (the rest went to the church). The pastor had a small cabin that Silas was able to make livable. There were other small jobs and improvements to the church, and inadvertently Silas again improved his skill set, now including basic carpentry and the fashioning of better nails.

Journey of a Slave from Plantation to Battlefield. *Library of Congress.*

But late in 1861, the pastor pulled Silas aside and told him that he was being rented to a factory in Richmond that made ammunition for the Confederate war effort. The explanation was surprisingly straightforward—the rates being paid to slave owners for their factory laborers was five times the amount that Silas could generate for the church in Augusta County. Silas would be helping the church, and he would be able to keep a slightly larger portion of the wages he earned for himself. In fact, he would even be able to choose his own living quarters if he made it through probation. The pastor made him scrawl his "X" on an affidavit that identified who his true owner was and to whom he was being leased. The pastor also pointed out that by signing he had agreed to extremely harsh penalties, up to and including death, if he breached any requirements of his employment. Silas inquired whether he could see his mother, friends and extended family back at the farm, and the pastor told him he could—as long as he made it to the five o'clock train in Staunton going to Richmond. Silas instinctively knew that there wasn't enough time.

When Silas arrived in Richmond, it was in the middle of the night, and gas lights lit up the streets, revealing a place that made Staunton look like a small town. Unlike Staunton, people were still busy in the middle of the dirty streets. Many African Americans, mainly men, were walking around openly, and Silas wondered if they were free or still in bondage. There were curfews back at home. He later found out there were curfews here, but apparently, they were not always enforced. He had the address of the Lutheran missionary house where he was told he could stay temporarily, and some of the men helped him toward it.

The work in the factory was similar to blacksmithing work he had done back in Augusta County. He worked beside many other African-American men who he found were mostly like him, slaves from other parts of Virginia who had been hired out by their masters. Some of them reported that they were living in shared quarters in the free African-American neighborhoods of Richmond, and soon Silas did this too. Some of the supervisors in the factory were free African Americans who lived in the same neighborhoods.

Silas wondered why the workers were not punished severely for being late or making mistakes. He was amazed when he was told that some owners had sent lawyers to the factory to demand that the workers not be abused. There was also a doctor who came to the factory once a month and offered voluntary medical checkups.

When after a few months this all seemed to be a normal routine, a white man in a gray uniform showed up at the factory, and Silas's name was one of many he called to come outside and stand in the courtyard. Several dozen of the men were informed that the Confederate States of America had rented out their services from their masters and that they were to form a work battalion digging earthworks and redoubts north of the city.

The work was difficult in the middle of the Virginia summer, and the overseer was another man in uniform who had no reluctance to strike the man who failed to work hard enough. The rations were moldy biscuits and rancid bacon, and the overseer insisted that they were better than what the average Confederate soldier was eating every day. Silas saw several men try to escape. Although it appeared that several made it, those who obviously didn't were tortured until near death. He again understood the same clear message.

After a few weeks of this, the remaining men (a few had died due to sunstroke, in addition to those who had escaped) were returned to the factory, presumably to resume their previous jobs. Silas, however, was called out and pulled aside by a white man with thin black mustache and an unfamiliar accent. He had a paper in his hand that he claimed was from the Lutheran church back in Augusta County asking that Silas be sold at market for the best possible price. Silas began to protest that William Franklin and the pastor would not do such a thing, that there must be some mistake. The man's response was to put chain shackles on his hands behind his back.

Silas ended up in a part of Richmond he had never seen, somewhere on the steep slopes east of the capitol, in a place that for all appearances was like a jail, complete with cells, iron bars and someone moaning nearby. The man with the mustache disappeared. Another man who appeared to be a doctor showed up and poked, prodded and examined Silas's teeth. Another showed up, made Silas strip down and then gave him some relatively new-looking homespun britches and a shirt.

Another showed up and moved Silas into the cell with the man who was moaning, apparently suffering from a beating. Silas knew that he was going to be sold. The next day, he was paraded out of the building and into a nearby structure that had a stage-like platform. The man with the mustache was there. When Silas's turn came, he was made to take his shirt off and stand on the stage. A number of white men raised their hands during the bidding, and apparently 1,500 Confederate dollars was a good price, for the man with a mustache nodded his head with satisfaction. Silas was hustled off to another courtyard, where he was shackled again and led to a short man in a black jacket and cravat. As he was loaded into the back of a wagon, the man with the cravat informed Silas that he was going to Caroline County and that "he was a damned expensive replacement for some incorrigible who had run away."

The plantation in Caroline County was not completely dissimilar to the farm near Staunton, although in this case, the slaves were treated quite differently. The owner had everyone under constant surveillance, and Silas was asked to report any unusual behavior on the part of any other slave. The other slaves were cool to him, and for the first time he could remember, Silas began to feel utterly alone. He noticed signs of severe abuse that he wasn't used to in his previous domiciles. He found out later that no one who had close relations remained on the property. The work was also grueling. For someone who had come to be justifiably proud of his craftsmanship and ingenuity, he was instead slopping hogs, topping tobacco and helping push a millstone that draft animals could have easily done.

There was little conversation between slaves or between the whites and the slaves. It was if a clock had not been rewound and time was standing still. Nothing was happening.

One morning, Silas arose and headed to the south of the field, where the male laborers gathered at dawn to receive their assignments. To his surprise, no one was there. A short distance away, he saw some figures dressed in blue standing near the master's house. He slowly headed that way until he could go no further without interacting with them. They were clearly Union soldiers, and they called him over.

"Where is everyone?" Silas asked.

"They went to eat the biggest breakfast they've had in a while," one soldier said.

Silas shook his head. "I don't understand."

"You're free, man! You are free! They went up the tracks to Guinea Station to get food. That's where our quartermaster is. Just follow the tracks north like they did." Silas hesitated. The soldiers seemed annoyed. "By the way, do you know where your master buried the family silver?" Silas shook his head. Then the soldiers ignored him. He paused for a long moment and wondered what was happening in Staunton. Then he turned around and headed toward the railroad tracks and north.

Silas Washington as a figure is a conglomerate fiction; each of the incidents is from real historical, documented occurrences showing the centrality of Richmond.[4]

FREE AFRICAN AMERICANS

Free African Americans were not actually free in the same sense that whites were. Richmond's roughly three thousand (actually probably much more by 1861) free African Americans were subject to restrictive laws that whites were not, and technically they could be forced to leave the state if the old laws still on the books were actually enforced. They were also subject to conscripted war labor, which many resisted through mostly passive methods—disappearing, losing paperwork, leaving worksites and so on. Many served only under threat of violence, laboring in salt mines, digging trenches, cutting wood or doing any of the many other things necessary to continue the war effort that would be impossible to accomplish with so many military-age men already in service to the army.

Free African Americans were required to carry proof of their status at all times, and in areas of contact between Union and Confederate forces, their behavior was subject to even more heightened scrutiny. A family living near the James River outside Richmond was evicted, for example, when they were suspected of giving aid or information to an enemy fleet in the area.

Chapter 3

RICHMOND COMMERCE BEFORE THE WAR

The antebellum economy of Richmond was considerably diverse, as a quick study of the annual business directories will indicate. From distilleries to dye production, what couldn't be made in the city was brought in on ships to Rockett's Landing from around the globe. The amazing diversity of people and products was one incentive in the early decision to move the Confederate capital from Montgomery, Alabama, to Richmond.

During the war, Rockett's Landing would become the center of the Confederate Navy Yard in Richmond. The same river that facilitated commerce and travel would become a chronic defense headache for authorities during the war. A second facility grew and expanded on the opposite south bank as the war progressed.

The geography of the city placed it in a unique position. The northeast course of the Blue Ridge Mountains meant that valley commerce flowed into the Potomac basin and ultimately to Washington, D.C., Baltimore and Philadelphia in addition to Richmond. To the south, Tidewater commerce could sail to ports like Wilmington, Charleston and Savannah. The advent of rail transportation meant that those same markets opened to Richmond, which had five separate rail lines by the start of the war. Richmond banks, brokers and industry thrived as significant amounts of goods and services flowed through the city.

Richmond began as an artisan town in the colonial era, founded by plantation owners who needed a port on the river to ship tobacco southeast

Wharf at Rockett's Landing (south side of James River). *Library of Congress.*

past Jamestown and to Europe via the Atlantic, as well as a center for ironsmiths, coopers and other services. As such, Richmond in 1860 was a successful tobacco city, perhaps considered the premier city of the business, with dozens of large warehouses, outbuildings and associated businesses. Production in Virginia remained steady into the war period, flowing through agents, buyers, wholesalers and shippers. In the 1860 city directory, for example, there are ninety-one separate tobacco business entities listed. No other large-scale industrial area could come close.

In 1860, there were 252 tobacco factories in Virginia. Of these, 109, as stated by the oldest manufacturers, were in Richmond, Petersburg, Lynchburg and Danville; the remaining 143 were distributed throughout the country districts and among the small towns. Of the thirty generally recognized tobacco counties, there were nineteen that could claim manufactories.[5]

TABLE 1. VIRGINIA ANTEBELLUM TOBACCO PRODUCTION (1810–1860)

YEAR	POUNDS
1619	40,000
1630	1,500,000
1750	51,800,000
1810	84,134,000
1820	83,940,000
1830	83,810,000
1840	119,484,000
1850	145,729,000
1860	167,274,000
1870	43,761,000
2016*	629,000,000*

*For comparison, this figure is for the entire United States

Sources: Encyclopediavirginia.org; encylopedia.com; accessgenealogy.com; *Virginia & Tobacco* (Tobacco Institute, 1960); worldatlas.com; 2000 United Nations Farm and Agricultural Output report; the Killebrew Reports (*Report on the Culture and Curing of Tobacco in the United States*, Killebrew, 1884); statista. com; *History of the Tobacco Industry in Virginia from 1860 to 1894*. The numbers were then compiled by the authors.

The importance of the tobacco industry on the eve of the Civil War to Richmond cannot be overstated. It likely directly or indirectly involved one in three laborers and slaves, or more. The ancillary businesses—those supporting the direct services—were even more varied (for example, clothiers for slaves and laborers, ship repair specialists and so on).

When the war started, the tobacco industry more or less collapsed for a number of complex reasons. The economy didn't absorb the loss evenly across areas of Virginia and the South. Tobacco was still grown, but the international and Northern markets quickly evaporated in the face of war and blockade. The tobacco infrastructure—slaves, tillable land, warehouses, agents—was quickly absorbed into other areas of the wartime economy. The war caused many tobacco warehouses to become prisons, tobacco fields to become corn or wheat fields, slaves to shift into factory work and agents to either be conscripted or find other similar work in another occupation.

View of the dock on South Side of James River opposite Rockett's Landing, April 1865. *Library of Congress.*

Richmond was also an international port city. Rockett's Landing, situated on the north bank of the James River below the fall line, was a deep-water facility that could receive even the largest ships of the pre–Civil War era. A deep-water port remains below Richmond even to the present day. As a result, there was an international flavor to Richmond that facilitated cultural and economic trade. The Confederate government later tried to take advantage of those connections to fight a war it was not prepared materially to engage in for the long term.

Richmond on the eve of the war was one of the East Coast's most vital ports. It was within easy reach of the U.S. Navy if Confederate authorities failed to act quickly. According to John Coski:

> *In 1860, 2,133 ships and boats arrived at the Richmond dock carrying such items as coal, fish, guano, hay, pig and scrap iron, salt, tar, and rosin, while 2,337 departed carrying 423,194 barrels of flour, 56,397 packages of tobacco, and 143,000 bushels of wheat. Even as late as December 1861, with the Federal blockade of the Southern coast in force, 109 commercial vehicles entered the Richmond dock.*[6]

Over time, especially after the coming of the railroads, Richmond began to become an iron and steel city. Although it had numerous small smithies, foundries and ironworks before the war, the Tredegar Iron Works, founded in 1837, became the embodiment of the modern capitalist industrial war complex.

The former main plant and environs are now a partnership between the Civil War museum and the National Park Service, called the American Civil War Museum. "One of the nation's most significant Civil War Sites, Tredegar is now a National Historic Landmark and is listed on the National Register of Historic Places and the Virginia Landmarks Register."

Richmond also spawned other forms of modern industry. The Gallego flour works had Richmond's first "skyscrapers," brick structures roughly ten stories high. Competing flour mills capitalizing on the railroads, canals and improved road system turned Richmond into the flour capital of the world for a period in the antebellum era. Ships took flour to South America and returned with coffee beans in their holds.

As state capital and a swiftly growing industrial center, Richmond also grew large numbers of supporting businesses, from high-end hotels to tiny

Tredegar Iron Works, about 1860. *Library of Congress.*

American Civil War Museum—Historic Tredegar. *Photo by Derek Kannemeyer.*

corner taverns. The city council spent much of its legislative time focused on monitoring gambling, prostitution, illegal bars and ruffian behavior. The social problems only grew worse during the war. For the ad-hoc merchants, the roiling human traffic meant the opportunity to make quick profits. There were, of course, many established restaurants, hotels and entertainments that enjoyed the official support of the town fathers. Some businesses may strike a modern reader as somewhat curious. For example, Richmond in 1860 had five guano (bat excrement) dealers.

Richmond also became a town of churches before the war, and although not technically part of commerce per se, they were an important glue that held the people engaged in commerce together. Many diverse denominations were represented, including but not limited to Methodists, Baptists, Catholics, Episcopalians and Quakers, as well as a Jewish synagogue (Beth Ahabah). In fact, the 1790 U.S. Census showed that Richmond had the fourth-largest Jewish population of any city in the new nation.

Richmond was a small business haven in 1860. The large amount of human traffic during legislative sessions, while seasonal, was less than the constant press of passengers, goods and railway workers at the various rail hubs in Richmond. In those days, rail cars could not be swapped because the gauge of the rails differed with each railroad. Cargo had to be unloaded from one train onto wagons and then reloaded onto another train for the rest of its journey. This flexibility meant that the economy could support increased specialization. The vitality of Richmond's commerce lured immigrants from Europe with specialized skills who continued to come to Richmond throughout the war.

The James River and Kanawha Canal was a grand idea that never quite lived up to expectations, but it ended up being surprisingly important to commerce and the military-industrial complex during the war. Established in 1785 through the efforts of George Washington, the goal was to extend the line of the James River with a canal navigable for flatbottom boats the entire way to the headwaters of the Kanawha River just east of present-day Charleston, West Virginia.

The effort suffered from numerous setbacks and difficulties, ranging from obstacles in the terrain to financial woes. In 1820, the state took over the corporation and started work back up. Work stalled again, and it wasn't until 1835 that the James River and Kanawha company formed and tried yet again. Under better civilian leadership and engineering, the canal was extended to Lynchburg and, by 1851, to Buchanan. It would never get any farther (196.5 miles) due to the difficulties of terrain, finance and the growth of railroads.

The canal competed with railroads in a losing battle but did, in fact, consist of an important link between Richmond and interior markets that would become even more critical during 1861–65. During the war, when the railroads were sorely overtaxed and even regular maintenance became impossible, the canal actually increased in strategic importance, and the government increasingly commandeered cargo space and built some of its own canalboats. Some private businesses also built their own private fleets. Chimborazo Hospital had its own boat and went to Lynchburg weekly for supplies.

Intimately tied to the fortunes of the tobacco industry, the canalboats known as bateaux were designed to hold a standard hogshead in width snugly within the open hold. There were other types of boats as well, designed to different purposes (such as moving people around). Between 1820 and 1840, there were hundreds of bateaux in service and more than 1,500 boat crew members (mostly free and enslaved African Americans). With the crash of the tobacco business in 1860–61, the canal industry, smartly, was ready to immediately switch over to government contracts and service related to the war economy. Combined with the breakdown of the railroad system over time, the canal remained more important than most people realized, bringing in everything from pig iron from Western Virginia to wheat from the Shenandoah Valley desperately needed by mills. During the Siege of Petersburg, with Lee's army desperately hungry, the canal traffic was particularly important.

The canal basin in downtown Richmond was situated between Eighth and Eleventh and Canal and Cary Streets. The "Great Basin," as it was known, was surrounded by factories, warehouses, merchants and myriad loading areas. It also served what trains would call a "turntable" function, where there was space for longer boats to turn around before heading back upriver. Historians have generally downplayed the importance of the canal to commerce and the war effort, but the records indicate that is not the case.

Chapter 4

THE WEST POINT BACKGROUND
OF THE GENERALS ON BOTH SIDES

The United States Military Academy trained the majority of officers and commanders on both sides of the conflict. Of the sixty biggest battles of the Civil War, West Point graduates commanded both armies in fifty-five. Of the remaining five, a West Point graduate commanded one of the opposing armies. What these leaders learned at West Point consisted mainly of the principles of engineering and administration of large forces but not how to engage large forces to fight. No Civil War commander had directed troops in any size, except maybe a regiment. Except for a few who fought in the Mexican-American War, none had even seen an army larger than fourteen thousand men. They read books and studied tactics since directors of the curricula did not believe that young cadets could benefit from studying strategy.

The strategy available to West Point instructors came from the writings of Antoine-Henri Jomini, who served with Napoleon and developed *The Art of War* (1838). The man who did the most to popularize Jomini in this country was Dennis Hart Mahan (father of Alfred Thayer Mahan, theorist of naval power), who began teaching at West Point in 1824. He was sent to Europe in 1826 to study and returned to West Point in 1830 after four years of studying Napoleonic warfare. He taught Jominian theory to a host of Civil War generals.

They were taught that in war, the rules of engagement mattered as much as human behavior. The key element of success for battle consisted of bringing the strength of your army to bear on the decisive point where the enemy was weakest. The other key to Jomini's principles focused on the primary objectives of his strategy, which stressed that places rather than armies were more important. He emphasized the seizure of "decisive strategic points" such as capitals. His operational strategy thus allowed the enemy the option of retiring from the field of battle, which might explain how Union generals allowed the Army of Northern Virginia to retreat several times after defeat on the battlefield rather than being decisively crushed. His principles looked backward into the eighteenth century and were based on what he observed during the Napoleonic War. His interpretations missed things that were new in favor of the continuation of conflict by more traditional methods. Those eighteenth-century principles emphasized maneuvers rather than battles. No wonder Lincoln, in particular, fretted over the actions, or lack thereof, from his generals until he arrived on Grant. Jomini formed his principles from times when armies were expensive to maintain and should not be risked unless victory was certain.

What Dennis Hart Mahan failed to teach cadets was the interconnectedness between war and the mechanics of war on the one hand and political objectives and national life on the other. In other words, the way Grant and Lincoln waged war after Grant took over the Eastern Theater bore no resemblance to the way generals conducted campaigns prior to March 2, 1864, when Lincoln revived the rank of lieutenant general and promoted Grant to that rank, along with making him general-in-chief, replacing Union general Henry W. Halleck. From this point on, the Confederacy faced Grant, Sherman and Philip Sheridan—the three best Union generals—all under the overall direction of Grant.

Adherence to the doctrines of Jomini caused the Union armies to miss opportunity after opportunity, even when they had the advantage to destroy Confederate armies during the first half of the war. Jomini's tenet that first an army must mass its forces with a preponderance of strength before advancing caused McClellan to idle the Army of the Potomac until he attained confidence in its power. Lincoln urged him over and over to take some action if for no other reason than to reassure the Northern public that the North possessed the capability to beat the Confederacy. Once, Lincoln was so frustrated at McClellan's failure to act that he sent the general a telegram that read, "If General McClellan does not want to use the Army, I would like to borrow it for a time, provided I could see how it could be made to do something."

Confederate generals were just as hidebound in their steadfastness to Jomini's precepts, but it showed less. Confederate commanders interpreted

Confederate commanders of the American Civil War, 1861–65. *Library of Congress.*

the Jomini canon differently. They solidly followed the principle of taking the offensive, especially Lee. Union troops had invaded the Confederates on their home soil! Unlike Union forces, Confederate armies were not tasked with taking and holding territory. Also, Mahan taught that speed and headlong attack would give an army a clear advantage. Confederate generals took that to heart. Lee more than any other general exhibited Jomini's principles. Lee showed how best to use Jomini's principles of

Opposite, top: Marching on Richmond. *From* Harper's History of the War, *Library of Congress.*

Opposite, bottom: General Lee's house during the war, 707 East Franklin. *Library of Congress.*

Right: General Lee's house today. *Photo by Derek Kannemeyer.*

exploiting the offensive, massing forces, economy of force, interior lines and unity of command. While Lee has been praised for his brilliance, he is best seen as a superior commander in a theater of war. He was not a strategic commander. T. Harry Williams said, "The Confederates, brilliant and bold executing Jominian strategy on the battlefield, never succeeded in lifting their gifts above the theater level." They were a product of their culture maintaining a local focus. What the Confederacy needed was for Lincoln and his generals to say that all the bloodshed and effort was not worth it. Since that never happened, this interpretation says the Confederacy would never attain its desire to be independent.

Williams noted that because of what so many generals on both sides internalized at West Point, they did not grow. In particular, Confederate commanders were the same men in 1865 as they had been in 1861. David Donald suggested that because of the South's early victories, its leadership saw less reason to change its strategy. In the end, Northern generals finally employed new methods of war. Many commanders were replaced by Lincoln over the course of the war. Then Grant and Sherman as a team forged a new approach to bring about the demise of the enemy, plus they had the resources of the North behind them. We cannot cover this topic here, but Grant had a skill set that was better adapted for a general waging a war on the home territory of his enemy. He does not appear to have felt restricted or confined by what he heard at West Point.

Chapter 5

BACKDROP OF THE SOUTH PRIOR TO 1860

After the American Revolution, the part of our nation we refer to as "the South" evolved into a different region from the rest of the country. Change was slow, but "the North" and "the South" saw each other differently by the mid-nineteenth century. The makeup of their respective populations began to differ. The North started to grow faster than the South, as immigrants settled more and more in the North. Shipping traffic most often docked at cities on the northern coast, creating a natural settlement destination where large immigrant groups could mingle with others from their native lands. The Irish congregated and lived among others of their nationality. Non-English-speaking immigrants had more reason to settle together. Ethnic settlements came to the South in much smaller numbers. Immigrants had no incentive to compete with their labor in a region where slavery was the dominant source of labor even in industry. In 1847, white workers went on strike to protest slaves being taught skilled trades at Tredegar Iron Works. Joseph Anderson, who ran the foundry, promptly told those workers they had fired themselves and told them to leave at once. It was tough to be any color under those conditions. But there were several other ironworks in the city at that time where these workers likely found employment. Therefore, by the mid-nineteenth century, the North had more immigrants and the South had larger native populations of both African American and white.

Virginia had some immigrants by the middle of the nineteenth century. There were notable immigrant populations of Germans in the Shenandoah

Valley from Pennsylvania. In Richmond by midcentury, there was a vibrant German community that made up more than 4 percent of the population according to the 1850 census. The tobacco trade attracted Germans, who exported mainly tobacco to Europe from Richmond. When those ships returned, they brought immigrants. The City of Bremen had established a consulate in Richmond by 1845. Other nations had consulates here as well. Included among these immigrants were a number of Jews especially from Bavaria who were fleeing the harsh restrictions on Jews in Germany. In the 1850 census, 1,284 Germans were counted. But northern cities had much larger concentrations of foreign-born citizens.

When we speak of people who lived in the middle of the nineteenth century, we must remember that their ideas were very different from our current worldview. It was, for example, a far more religious time for America. Here again the differences between the North and the South that would separate our nation made their first appearance. Richmond and other parts of Virginia and the South experienced disunion first within the denominations where people worshiped.

After about 1830, more and more Christians began to push for the abolition of slavery. There was a great revival of religious fervor, especially in the North. As a result, southern churches became more defensive about their beliefs, and preaching tended to support slavery. The first break occurred when various denominations refused to appoint slaveholders as missionaries. For example, at the Methodist General Conference of 1844, delegates from the North refused to recognize the authority of a slaveholding bishop. Southern churches were already upset at preaching that declared that slavery was not a part of Christian doctrine. In 1844, southern Methodists broke with their convention and created a Southern Methodist Convention. In 1845, the Baptists formed the Southern Baptist Convention. Religious differences played out within many congregations as well, especially in areas that later favored the Union in towns such as in Leesburg, Warrenton and Fredericksburg. Every major denomination split along regional lines so that by the time secession came up for discussion, the church already lived in a house divided.

"But in the end," as George Brown Tindall said, "what made the South distinctive was its people's belief, and other people's belief, that they were distinctive." Agriculture dominated the economy of the South. Southerners saw themselves as the heirs of the nation that sought independence, so that when the idea of secession arose, they felt at some level that they were defenders of freedom, even though slaves were denied their freedom.

The South had more military colleges and schools and extolled guns and fighting more than the North.

Other signs and portents of the widening differences between the two parts of the nation had appeared by midcentury. The North was more industrialized than the South. The North expanded public education much more rapidly than the South. In 1850, only 80 percent of the white population in the South was literate, and only 10 percent of slaves could read, which was prohibited in most areas anyway. Children attended school on average for six months in the North but only three months in the South, and of course, no schools for slaves existed. The North had more banks, more railroads and better roads and bridges. The North's focus on free-labor industrial capitalism made the institution of slavery seem more and more out of sync with the times. However, slavery had enabled cotton production to soar between 1800 and 1860 such that the South produced three-quarters of the world's supply of cotton. All of these factors created tangible rifts in the economy and intangible rifts in the minds of citizens in both regions.

The split became pronounced when Congress debated an appropriation for Polk's proposed Mexican-American War on a hot and humid Washington, D.C., Saturday night of August 8, 1846. David Wilmot, a first-term representative from Pennsylvania, attached an amendment to the bill. It noted "that, as an express and fundamental condition of the acquisition of any territory from the Republic of Mexico…neither slavery nor involuntary servitude shall ever exist in any part of said territory." Northern Democrats, who were not totally antislavery but had other grievances against the Polk administration, joined with northern Whigs to pass this measure over the united opposition of southern Democrats and southern Whigs. This was a huge blow to the South's political power and the existing tacit agreement to maintain a balance between slave and free territory as the nation expanded westward. However, Congress adjourned before it could be brought to the Senate, where it would have met certain defeat since fifteen slave states held the majority there. In the fall session, the administration convinced enough Democrats to drop the Wilmot provision from the bill, and the bill ultimately passed. President Polk in his diary recognized the writing on the wall. He wrote that the implications of political realignment could "ultimately threaten the Union itself." These were the clouds forming over Richmond, the South and the entire nation.

LINCOLN'S ELECTION

The period from 1850 to 1860 contains too much narrative for us to even attempt to summarize. The election of Abraham Lincoln in November 1860 galvanized those called fire-eaters in the South to act forcefully. South Carolina acted first. The South Carolina legislature called a convention to deal with the issue of secession that on December 20, 1860, voted 169 to 0 to secede from the Union. By February 1, six additional states had seceded: Mississippi, Florida, Alabama, Georgia, Louisiana and Texas. Within three months of Lincoln's election, these states had seceded from the Union, set up a capital in Montgomery, Alabama, drafted a constitution and formed the Confederate States of America. Think of the lines that form in our day outside of some stores on Black Friday. When the doors open, there is an inexorable push from the back of the crowd. That's what happened across the South in the spring of 1861. Everyone wanted in on secession. It reached Richmond and Virginia later than states farther south. South Carolina set off a domino effect that other states followed. Four years later, Sherman purposely burned Columbia, South Carolina, to punish the state for having set the war in motion.

PART II

RICHMOND AND VIRGINIA, 1861–1864

Chapter 6

SECESSION AND THE NEW CAPITAL
OF THE CONFEDERACY

F ort Sumter, still under construction, was fired on by Confederate forces on April 12, 1861. The small garrison there surrendered on April 14. The next day, Lincoln declared his intention to put down the insurrection with troops from every loyal state. Other slave states had to decide right then where they stood. Virginia had been a primarily Union-leaning state up to that point. The Virginia secession convention had debated the issue, but no clear consensus had emerged. The territory that today makes up West Virginia was part of Virginia, with delegates at the convention meeting in Richmond. They had no desire to leave the Union, and slavery was not part of the agricultural makeup in those mountainous counties.

Virginia's governor, John Letcher, did not desire that Virginia leave the Union. Richmond had little in common with the radical agrarian viewpoint of the Cotton South. But forced to choose between leaving the Union and joining forces to wage war on states that had already seceded forced Virginia's hand. Many rallies and marches had taken place in favor of secession already. The secession convention, having debated the issue for two months, voted to secede on April 17, 1861. On May 7, the existing Confederate Congress admitted Virginia to the Confederacy, even though the popular vote had not yet approved the motion for secession (it did so finally on May 23). Three other states in the Upper South—Tennessee, North Carolina and Arkansas—very quickly joined the CSA.

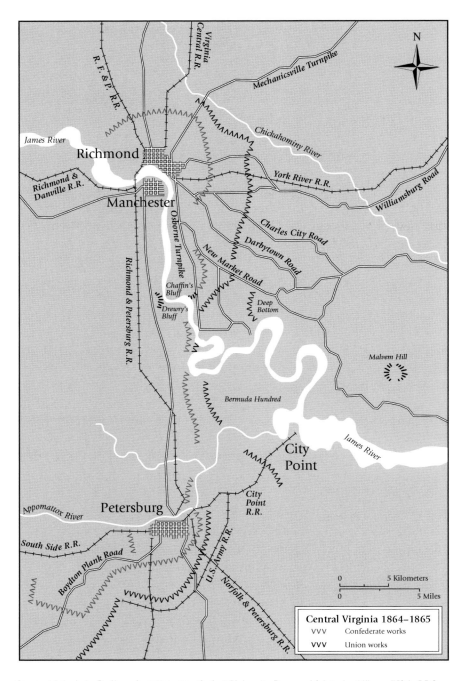

Central Virginia Railroads, 1861–65. *Oxford University Press and Maps by Alliance USA, LLC.*

Why Richmond Became Capital
of the Confederacy

The Secession Convention of Virginia invited the Confederacy to make Richmond its capital because, first, it would put the administration of the war closer to what would likely be the Eastern Theater of war and, second, Richmond would be strongly defended to protect railroad hubs and manufacturing. On Wednesday, April 17, the Virginia Secession Convention voted eighty-eight to fifty-five to secede. The forty-nine delegates from the western part of the state that later became West Virginia voted seventeen in favor, thirty nay and two abstentions. Meanwhile, during the spring of 1861, news arrived that the Confederate Congress approved Richmond as the capital on May 20, even before the popular vote by Virginians consented to secede. Jefferson Davis arrived in Richmond on May 29 to great celebrations. As soon as delegates from the far western counties (present-day West Virginia) returned home, they organized a convention in Wheeling to decide if they wished to remain in the Union. Ultimately, those western counties voted to secede from Virginia and applied for statehood to the U.S. Congress. West Virginia was admitted to the Union on June 20, 1863, after it inserted a provision for the abolition of slavery into its constitution.

Besides Virginia, it was critical for the CSA to include North Carolina and Tennessee as well. These three states were the three most populous states in the Confederacy. Atlanta had only 9,544 inhabitants in 1860 according to the census. Virginia, North Carolina and Tennessee produced more than half of all food crops and produced half of all horses and mules in the South. The original seven Confederate states could not have lasted four years without these big three. Finally, Richmond contained 40 percent of all manufacturing capacity in 1861. No wonder it became the capital.

Richmond churches supported secession. Reverend Moses D. Hoge, pastor of Second Presbyterian Church, declared in June 1861, "We are menaced with subjugation for daring to assert the right to self-government." Other voices and the euphoria around war talk in a region dependent on the use of guns and reverence for the military drowned out any other voices, such as Governor Lechter's, that would urge caution.

On the other hand, this united focus enabled the rapid establishment of a brand-new country—post office, currency, defense, seat of government, legislature and buildings to house all these functions. Certainly, many offices and heads of departments for the CSA were quickly laid out, but

Right: The Honorable Chester Dorman Hubbard of West Virginia, delegate to Virginia Convention at Richmond in 1861 (opposed secession). *Library of Congress.*

Below: State capitol building, Richmond, Virginia, April 1865. *Library of Congress.*

Confederate brass mountain howitzers on streets of Richmond, Virginia. *Library of Congress.*

the infrastructure to oversee those needed functions had to be created. The army quickly formed along with the War Department as cabinet members moved from Montgomery, Alabama, to Richmond. Private citizens stepped up to fill gaps. According to Emory M. Thomas, "Fifty prominent citizens, most past military age, formed the Richmond Ambulance Corps to assist the wounded." Churches formed ad hoc uniform depots, where they collected fabric and accessories to make uniforms. The Confederate government soon took over all these functions, but churches continued to supply bandages and socks during the war.

None of this could have happened without able, energetic and driven men and many women stepping up to make the CSA a viable nation.

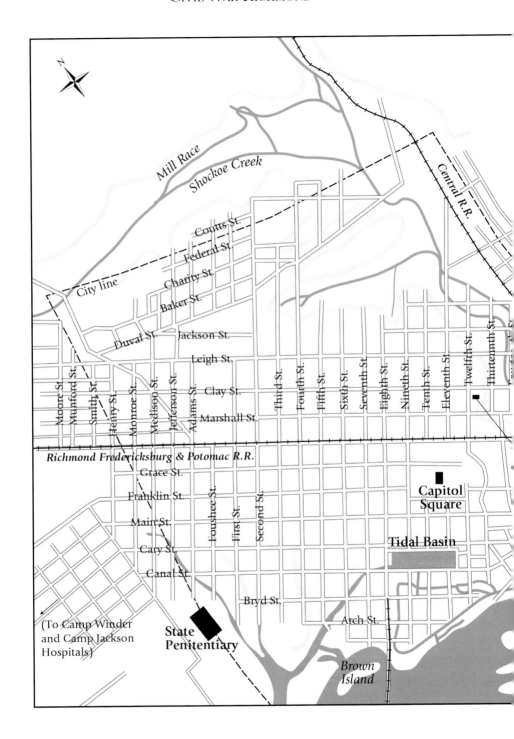

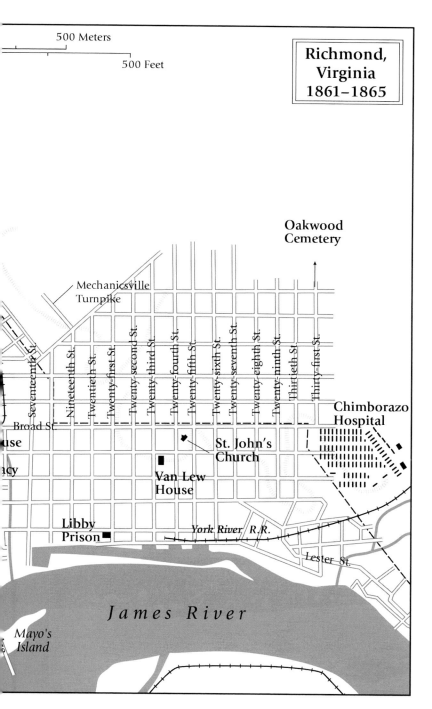

500 Meters

500 Feet

Richmond,
Virginia
1861–1865

Oakwood
Cemetery

Mechanicsville
Turnpike

Seventeenth St.

Nineteenth St.

Twentieth St.

Twenty-first St.

Twenty-second St.

Twenty-third St.

Twenty-fourth St.

Twenty-fifth St.

Twenty-sixth St.

Twenty-seventh St.

Twenty-eighth St.

Twenty-ninth St.

Thirtieth St.

Thirty-first St.

Chimborazo
Hospital

Broad St.

St. John's
Church

Van Lew
House

Libby
Prison

York River R.R.

Lester St.

James River

Mayo's
Island

Oxford
University
Press and
Maps by
Alliance
USA, LLC.

Left: John Letcher, governor of Virginia. *Library of Congress.*

Right: Second Presbyterian Church, Fifth Street. *Photo by Derek Kannemeyer.*

Suddenly over a few years, in a city of thirty-seven thousand, a government formed that eventually employed many thousands. It was the same phenomenon that our nation experienced when the advent of World War II pulled the nation out of the Great Depression. Due to the significant rise in manufacturing to supply the army, even slaves got the opportunity to become workers at manufacturers such as Tredegar Iron Works. Slaves could live on their own. Free African Americans, chronically underemployed, found some work building fortifications for the city because for others the pay was so low. Many men got the chance to serve as officers, providing administration over those under their command. It provided experience that would prove beneficial, as former military officers ran businesses that returned the city to prosperity after the war. Men such as Lieutenant Peter C. Mayo and Major Lewis Ginter re-created Richmond's tobacco industry in the 1870s. The frightful conflict created opportunities for men such as Ulysses S. Grant and Robert E. Lee to achieve victories that made them eternally famous. The

South achieved as much as it did because society was opened up in a manner that allowed talents to emerge in ways that might not have been available had the issue of slavery been resolved in some other fashion. Richmond even benefited in a strange way from the nostalgia of being the capital of the Confederacy and the seat of the Lost Cause.

Chapter 7

IMPACT OF THE WAR ON THE POPULATION

Many sources indicate that the city's population doubled in 1861. Sallie Brock Putnam (she did not become Mrs. Putnam until she married after the war) cited people fleeing the uncertainty of where they lived for the relative safety of Richmond. Also, after First Manassas, many wounded soldiers came to Richmond, along with Union prisoners. Wives and mothers of soldiers also came by the hundreds to nurse wounded sons and husbands. Even the wives of prisoners came to do the same for their loved ones, if allowed. There were many reasons to come to Richmond, including economic benefit. Combined with all of the government offices and army personnel, there were as many as 100,000 people or more in the city area at any given time. By the middle of the war, the population would exceed 100,000 people, making it the tenth-largest city in North America just behind Chicago.

The increase in population had several specific sources. First, once the provisional government in Montgomery was replaced by Richmond, all of the cabinet members and legislators, consisting of 132 senators and representatives, many with their families, moved here. They met for varying periods, most likely using hotels as lodging for four years. Second, members and their families of the executive branch and the Departments of State, War, Navy, Treasury and Justice, plus the Confederate Post Office, arrived next. These departments required bureau chiefs, assistant chiefs, clerks of varying levels of skills, aides, messengers and many other functionaries. These departments grew as the war progressed. Since telegraph was still

Spotswood Hotel, 1861, Eighth and Main Streets. *Library of Congress.*

in its infancy and telephones did not exist, messenger services flourished. Officials often stayed at the Spotswood Hotel.

An interesting feature of wartime life in Richmond had to do with the layers of bureaucracy and authority that overlapped. There was a federal authority that used Richmond as its headquarters (Confederate States of America), a state government (Richmond being Virginia's capital), a city government including mayor and council (Richmond) and even smaller jurisdictions within the city—headquarters of various civic and business organizations, plus religious denominations. In summary, a decision made about something in Richmond usually emanated from the proper city authority. But in more cases than anyone would have wished, there were often conflicting agendas, questions of authority and competition across all of the various bureaucratic layers.

For example, various city authorities arrested disorderly persons and dealt with them within the purview of their authority but may have had to defer to another jurisdiction, as in this case reported in the *Dispatch* on November 24, 1862: "The under mentioned soldiers, taken by the Watch, were sent to Castle Thunder to be returned to their regiments: Harman L. Seay, drunk and sitting on the street; Charles Alexander, drunk and lying on the sidewalk; Wm. Masengale, John Robertson, and Henry Mitchell, for disorderly conduct in the Varieties theatre." Reference in the newspapers to "The Cage" was possibly the Henrico County Jail, a holding jail for those who would shortly go into the Richmond Court and face the wrath of Mayor Mayo. It was heavily used during the Civil War.

THE MINDSET OF THE PEOPLE IN RICHMOND

Organized religion was always a big factor in the life of Richmonders, but the psychological pressures of the war made people emphasize their beliefs even more. When the institution of slavery came under attack prior to the war, more and more ministers preached sermons that supported slavery with references to numerous verses that supported subjugation to masters. After secession, sermons promised that the Lord was on the side of the South. Organized religion took the viewpoint that they were engaged in a struggle for independence, supported by references to the American Revolution, and that therefore victory would come to the Confederacy ultimately. Sallie Brock Putnam wrote, "The Richmond pulpit is filled by men of a superior order of talent, of the finest and most varied style of oratory, and of unquestionable piety and integrity." They took their calling so seriously that one minister, Moses D. Hoge of Second Presbyterian Church, obtained 300,000 Bibles from England on a blockade runner to distribute across the land.

Most Richmond churches experienced an increase in membership. But religious groups that did not support the Confederate cause, such as the Quakers, kept a low profile. The city's pulpits continually espoused the need for continuous sacrifice to support the cause. When casualties began to pour into Richmond, churches organized their members to provide support for the hospitals. Churches also provided important venues to mourn those who died in the fight.

Civil War envelope showing the Confederate Stars and Bars over cannons with patriotic verse. *Library of Congress.*

CIVILIAN WORKFORCE

The Treasury and War Departments were the largest bureaucracies. By 1864, there were more than five hundred Treasury employees, according to historian Stephen Ash. Every piece of currency had to have official signatures and stamps, even as its value declined. The War Department encompassed not only the command structure of the Confederacy but also all the supporting infrastructure, including quartermaster, hospitals, prisons and army facilities. These functions had to be overseen in the Western Theater from New Orleans to Vicksburg, Tennessee. Similar infrastructure supported Confederate troops in the Eastern Theater as well. Opportunities for employment in the CSA and industries supporting the war changed society like never before.

Thousands of troops came to the city to be processed, trained and assigned to various units where they would fight. In early 1862, a training camp, Camp Lee, was established west of the city north of Broad Street roughly covering the present Redskins Training Camp. A rail line shuttled troops from the city to the camp, creating constant activity. Additionally, the creation of a garrison to defend the city required administration.

Although Richmond was a powerful economic center for the war effort and fledgling rebel government, unreasonable demands on the infrastructure

Figure 1

Functions of the War Department

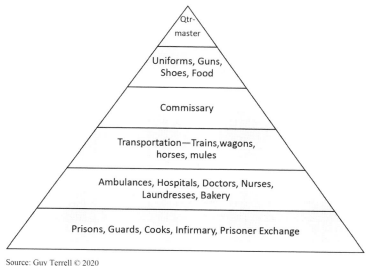

Source: Guy Terrell © 2020

were quickly made apparent, creating inflation and deprivation. Rail lines and rolling stock deteriorated from heavy use, but iron went primarily to the war effort; record harvests came in from the Valley and other regional farmers, but foodstuffs largely went to the army; and wartime profiteering made fortunes for some, while widows and wounded soldiers struggled to find the basic necessities. Over time, the economy began to deteriorate, and the population increasingly suffered.

The strained economy, coupled with the transitory nature of the city's population, meant that entertainment sometimes was limited to what people could come up with at home or among groups of friends. Children were particularly resourceful, as toy production (and purchase) was not the highest of Confederate priorities. According to the Delta Cultural Center, most games required little of value but lots of ingenuity. Such games included pick-up sticks, marbles (easily made from local clay), an indoor version of bowling sometimes called "ninepins" (and easily adapted to common wooden floors) and cup-and-ball, along with small toys like yo-yos and tops that could be fashioned from scrap wood or other cheap material.

For adults, entertainment could be formal (theater, circus, oratory) or informal (cards, charades or dancing). As the war progressed, entertainment of a formal nature became a luxury solely for the rich. Most middle class and underclass Richmonders could barely afford rent and food, let alone a trip to the opera or theater. Fairs were one notable exception, since one could often walk around, greet people and take in the exhibits, sometimes without having to pay an entrance fee.

HAUNTED RICHMOND

It's not unusual for a population under stress to experience or report more paranormal events than usual (unexplained by conventional science). Residents in Richmond reported many unusual happenings during the war, ranging from bedside appearances of loved ones who died in battle to hearing the sounds of battle occurring hundreds of miles away.

One famous Civil War story involves the cast-iron statue of a dog that resided in front of a general goods store on Broad Street. The legend tells of a little girl who loved the dog as if it were real and visited it regularly, but she died of scarlet fever and was interred at Hollywood Cemetery. The statue was moved to the cemetery, and people then reported seeing a ghostly dog (not just the statue) guarding her grave. The reality is that Charles Reese bought the statue for his children and had it moved to avoid it being melted down for the war effort, but the story lives on (and the dog statue is still in the cemetery).

It was common in the war period for people to experience visitations from those recently deceased. Mary Chesnut recalled in her diary:

> *Footprints on the boundaries of another world once more. Willie Taylor, before he left home for the army, fancied one day—day, remember—that he saw Albert Rhett standing by his side. He recoiled from the ghostly presence. "You need not do that, Willie. You will soon be as I am." Willie rushed into the next room to tell them what had happened, and fainted. It had a very depressing effect upon him. And now the other day he died in Virginia.*

Many of Richmond's most famous ghost stories date from the antebellum and Civil War era. Given the tremendous stress and social upheaval—and the amount of death—it is no wonder. See Haunts of Richmond (https://www.hauntsofrichmond.com) for tours that visit Civil War sites.

PSYCHOLOGICAL IMPACTS ON CIVILIANS

Because of Richmond's proximity to the enemy capital, Washington, D.C., citizens were in a constant state of anxiety about invasion. In particular, Union forces could move by naval transport fast enough that they might show up any day at Rockett's Landing or south of the falls. Batteries were established along the heights of the lower river, such as at Drewry's Bluff. Construction of ironclads and conversion of other steam vessels were expedited with the limited resources on hand. The navy was usually a distant second place to the army, which had orders for everything from armored train cars to heavy field artillery with local industry.

Although the city was only in serious danger on a few occasions, events occurred during the war that fed this steady anxiety (Seven Days Battles, Drewry's Bluff, Dahlgren's Raid and more). Even with telegraph and some access to enemy newspapers, Richmonders didn't really know when the threat would actually come to fruition. This constant anxiety was tiring for the population and almost certainly contributed to an increase in crime, suicide, alcoholism and other social problems.

The February/March 1864 operation against Richmond by General Judson Kirkpatrick and his subordinate Colonel Ulric Dahlgren did come closer than many knew at the time to taking Richmond by storm. It failed, resulting in Dahlgren's death and the discovery of papers on his body purportedly planning the assassination of Jefferson Davis and his cabinet. Of equal interest, it shows that Lee may have made the first known use of photo copies in American history. According to George E. Pond:

> *A fortnight later, General R.E. Lee sent to General Meade photographic copies of the two documents, with a letter making the extracts already quoted with their context, and requesting to know whether these alleged designs and instructions of Colonel Dahlgren were authorized by the United States Government, or by his superior officer, or were now approved by them.*[7]

A detailed description of the Dahlgren affair may be found in Elizabeth Varon's book, *Southern Lady, Yankee Spy*, where the extreme efforts of Unionists saved the body of Dahlgren from a secret grave, showing the reverence of most Southerners for a good death. The press used these papers to show how low the Union would go avoiding the normal "rules" of war. Scholars today say that the papers were in keeping with Union aspirations to strike a definitive blow to the Confederate government. They were not just a propaganda effort by the CSA aimed at generating sympathy for its cause.

WHERE PEOPLE FOUND HOUSING

About one thousand civil servants came to Richmond from Montgomery with the initial newly formed Confederacy. They all needed a place to live, plus their families had to be housed. Then many seeking employment came to Richmond. The burgeoning capital attracted adventurers as well as entrepreneurs. Military units from other states on the way to the army added to the city's population if only for a short time. Once the war began, people fled areas that came under control of the Union, such as Norfolk. After the First Battle of Bull Run (Union name for First Manassas), prisoners and the wounded had to be housed. Many relatives of prisoners and wounded also came to Richmond. Change occurred so rapidly that finding shelter put both the city and its citizens under severe stress.

Houses in Richmond have always been constructed close together. This was true even in the early part of the nineteenth century before the war. Families wanted to live as close to shopping and work as possible even then, especially since everyone mostly walked. The houses were typically two- or three-story brick homes. They were close together, with a kitchen outbuilding behind the main house, often with a place for a servant or slave to live. Photographic evidence supports these statements, as do casual walks in older parts of the city even today. These trends continued even as the city rebuilt and grew after the war. Housing farther out from the city center had larger lots, so less chance of fire, and could then be built of wood, which was cheaper than brick. The influx of inhabitants after 1861 did not create a housing boom because of a shortage of building materials and labor. Many laborers had joined the army, and many military facilities had to be constructed, especially hospitals. Sawmills were hard pressed to provide all the lumber for military contracts. One of the most severe shortages was nails. The Old Dominion Iron and Nail Works, located on Belle Isle, could not keep up with the demand for its products from both the army and the navy, which built a shipyard, ordnance laboratory and other facilities. The army and navy contracts similarly swallowed up any African-American skilled tradesmen since the white builder tradesmen had enlisted or were likewise under contract. These factors caused the price of a keg of nails to go from $4.50 to $175 by the end of 1864.

What people did to find housing was simply to double up or worse. Anyone inclined to rent rooms to boarders did so. Many converted family parlors from daytime use into bedrooms at night. By March 1862, every room was taken. There were no apartments as we might think of them. Additionally, if your room had a broken window, there was no glass to repair it, and rooms were frightfully cold in winter. Rent took almost all of a person's pay. Needless to say, rents moved skyward as inflation affected every commodity. It was hard to be in Richmond. Those who lived in comfort before the war inevitably suffered whether they were landlord or tenant.

The alternative required living in a nearby county or other place outside the city, such as Ashland, where a civil servant could take the RF&P train to Richmond each day, but whatever accommodations a person secured, it required hours in travel, much like some of today's commutes. Some government or office workers slept in their offices at night. Some hospitals set up dormitories, with surgeons and doctors' rooms on one side of a building and nurses and matrons on the opposite side. These were newly constructed buildings with unpainted wooden walls. New wood gives off an odor that not everyone finds pleasant.

For the rest, the city's poorest inhabitants, small, free-standing shanties were home. These could be cobbled together from scrap materials, but even that must have been hard to find as shortages of every kind increased. Stephen Ash retold the story of a twenty-two-year-old prostitute named Parmelia Robertson who died in October 1863 in the vicinity of Rockett's Landing. The *Dispatch* reported that she lived in "a miserable hovel about twelve by fourteen feet in size, the front used as a doggery [a cheap saloon] and the rear occupied as a lodging room" with two other women. The coroner said she killed herself with an overdose of laudanum.

The city, even during the most trying times, maintained a poorhouse where those with mental illness or who were homeless or simply passing through Richmond found some lodging. Orphans from other cities were found here as they tagged along with army units headed to the front. The war produced many sad souls who had lost their families.

CRIME

With such a large increase in population so quickly, new people perhaps had less regard for previous customs and practices than those who were born in Richmond. Richmond became a more dangerous city to live in during the war. In addition to the population explosion, the nature of a transient community, with thousands of refugees and soldiers on temporary leave, meant that crime increased dramatically, from assault and theft to murder and other disturbing crimes. Fewer people knew one another. Locals complained with repetitive entries in diaries and letters about gamblers, prostitution, drunkenness, assault, theft and vandalism. It was common for glass panes that were broken to not be replaced and instead be stuffed with old linen or covered with paper, an ineffective technique no matter the season.

Boys became a bigger problem during the war. Normally socialized by fathers with a trade, mothers with time and attention and sometimes schools that educated them, they were instead loosed on the streets of Richmond to wreak a different kind of havoc. There had been boy gangs before the war, but they grew in intensity during the war (and continued into the early twentieth century.) They each claimed dominion over areas of the city. They were bare-fisted, prank-pulling, brick-throwing hooligans. They called one another "cats" as a pejorative at first, but it stuck. The two best known were the Shockoe Hill Cats and the Butchertown Cats.

The Mayor's Court (Joe Mayo) reads like a list of all the petty and evil things humans are capable of:

1860-10-30, Richmond Dispatch*; John Gorman, sailor on USS Brooklyn passes out drunk and taken to the Mayor who lets him go.*

1860-12-25, Richmond Dispatch*; two men assault and beat a woman at the corner of 7th and Cary streets.*

1861-03-19, Richmond Dispatch*; "Disorderly boys" at Stewart's school House, Clay street, between 5th and 6th (future Samaritan Hospital). Boys are "in the habit of throwing stones at people, breaking windows, and being 'sassy' generally."*

1861-06-13, Richmond Dispatch*; man brought in to Mayor's court for allegedly keeping his bar open past ten o'clock.*

1861-09-10, Richmond Whig*; description of a rock battle between the "Shockoe Hill Cats" and "Butcher Cats," and the police raid that stopped it*

1861-09-27, Richmond Enquirer*; interesting Mayor's Court items: one of the combatants in the "Hill cats/Butcher cats" rock battle unable to prove his good character, and a slave assaults a "free negress."*

1861-11-08, Richmond Enquirer*; A guard at Louisiana Hospital accidentally shot a fellow guard.*

General Winder before joining Confederacy. *Library of Congress.*

General Samuel Winder was provost marshal for much of the war and had the unenviable task of keeping military order, but he also breached the gaps between civilian authorities and military authorities, of which there were countless instances. He died before the end of the war, and his reputation remains controversial to this day.

Some sociologists believe that experiences like these are more likely to occur or be noticed during great times of stress. Richmond was often palpably under duress from the threat of Union armies together with the constant influx of dying or wounded soldiers, besides the economic stress of want and hardship as the war continued. It's no wonder that it seemed as if the visible and invisible worlds were both fraying. Everyday life was increasingly interrupted by death. Mary Chesnut wrote about the first of many funerals:

> *Witnessed for the first time a military funeral. As that march came wailing up, they say Mrs. Bartow fainted. The empty saddle and the led war-horse—we saw and heard it all, and now it seems we are never out of the sound of the Dead March in Saul. It comes and it comes, until I feel inclined to close my ears and scream.*

Entertainment

The Seabrook tobacco warehouse (north side of Grace between Seventeenth and Eighteenth), opened in 1810 by John Seabrook, was later acquired by the city and became General Hospital No. 9 during the war. The building was also known as "Richmond's billboard" since it was commonly peppered with posters, waybills and political ads. Even though a war was on, the need for entertainment in the crowded city was probably greater than ever, and one place to find out about it besides the newspapers was a walk by the "papered" hospital.

Richmonders were already used to the typical menu of antebellum entertainments that many Americans enjoyed, ranging from classic theater to traveling circuses, band concerts, balls (early in the war), horse races and, of course, any number of parades and military-oriented fairs that proliferated once the war started. Much of entertainment turned to the dual purpose of supporting the war effort:

> *THE HENNINGSEN HOSPITAL.—We are requested to say that a trotting race will take place over Waggoner's track this afternoon at three o'clock, for the benefit of the Henningsen Hospital.*[8]

Sometimes culture, entertainment and sport, when mixed with alcohol, turned ugly. The number of incidents of drunkenness, brawling and disorderly conduct skyrocketed as the war went on. But the need for entertainment never diminished, no matter how grim the economy or war news became.

The New Marshall Theatre was built in 1862 (the old one, erected in 1819, burned down in December 1861), required more than 2.5 million

Drewry's Bluff, 1865. *Library of Congress.*

bricks and included four impressive Corinthian columns at the front of the structure. "Every door on the outside [front] will be illuminated with glass lamps, protected by wire netting," the Richmond *Dispatch* reported. "There are ten outside doors to the building. It will be ready for occupancy about the middle of January." The new theater could hold up to 650 occupants.

As odd as it sounds, Americans on both sides engaged in what one might call today "military tourism," sometimes paying to see military facilities, battlefields, new military inventions and important sites. In 1862, for example, a company started offering one dollar round trips down the James River from Richmond to see the facilities and dramatic terrain at Chaffin's and Drewry's Bluff, where the Confederate naval forces (fighting on land) and army had turned away the Union fleet. The cost also covered the return trip. Later, a company offered moonlit trips to the same location.

The Richmond *Dispatch* announced on March 20, 1861, designs for a new opera house mid-war:

> *Opera House.—A number of citizens have united in the design to establish in the city of Richmond an opera house. Sixty thousand dollars have already been subscribed, and as much more, it is said, can be made available for the purpose. The lot on the corner of 8th and Main streets, opposite the Spotswood Hotel, and the vacant one on Broad street, adjoining 8th, are talked of as the sites on which the proposed building shall be erected.*

Many Richmonders distracted themselves with reading, and while there wasn't necessarily a shortage of books relative to the start of the war, the dramatic increase in population and severe shortage of paper meant that publishers had to continually raise prices, and there eventually was a shortage of sorts. The publishers West and Johnson, for example, made a public apology to their subscribers for raising prices on the soon coming edition of *Les Misérables* due to the chronic lack of paper and related materials.

Some Richmonders left the city for entertainment. The hamlet of Ashland just north of the city (later the relocation spot for Randolph-Macon College) had a racetrack and a few outbuildings, but soon during the war it became an escape spot for entertainment, drinking, betting, racing and socializing. The RF&P rail line coming out of Richmond led directly there. When a "hop" was held in Ashland in 1864, an extra train was organized to handle the traffic.

Some forms of entertainment were not as socially acceptable among certain classes. Cockfighting, as reported in the *Whig* on January 2, 1865, was a popular activity for some:

> THE COCK FIGHT.—*The great cock fight between the game stock of Messrs. Duke & Gilmour, was brought to a conclusion yesterday, at the cock-pit in the yard of Omohundro's jail, near Seabrook's hospital, in the presence of several hundred lovers of the sport. Six battles were fought, Mr. Duke winning every one. The first fight was one of the most remarkable on record. It was between a Dusty Miller of Mr. Gilmour's and a red cock known as Bill Bailey, belonging to Mr. Duke. It lasted over two hours.— For the first hour, the Dusty Miller, who was by four ounces the heavier, was the general favorite, but Billy out winded his bulky antagonist and killed him. This is the first instance where one man has been known to win every fight of a main. The company present were of the same select description as on the previous day, and everything went off charmingly. Much money and apple brandy changed hands.*

Even immediately after the evacuation (April 2) and surrender (April 9), entertainment remained in the news. On April 18, 1862, it was announced that a minstrel troupe from Baltimore would very shortly be coming to the Metropolitan Hall to entertain city dwellers.

Chapter 8

THE CITY AS A SUPPLY AND MANUFACTURING CENTER

Richmond was already as industrialized as any city in the South (and many in the North, falling just outside the top ten in some lists), but it would become a unique early example of modern urban militarization and growth of the industrial complex. In fact, the 1861 Confederate economy was on par with major European nations such as Germany and Italy. Although it did suffer a number of significant paucities in comparison to the North (e.g., railroad mileage 22,000 in the North to 9,500 in the South), placed in the context of the time it is somewhat problematic to consider the CSA a purely agricultural nation in the pre-industrial sense. Great Britain, for example, had 10,400 miles of railway in 1860, roughly the same as the South/CSA. The big problem in the South was that railroads were small, usually one hundred miles or less, and each railway had its own gauge track. It was as if each railroad were a separate nation.

Later in the war, Confederate forces captured Union locomotives and had to use Tredegar and other foundries to convert them to the proper gauge for Southern lines. This was apparently the only source of new engines during the war for the CSA, as there are no records of newly constructed engines in the South after 1860–61.

William G. Thomas also pointed out that much of the Southern rail itself was relatively new. Much of the industrial infrastructure was new. This also was an advantage typically not recognized. Industry was rapidly expanding in the South in 1860 and only accelerated more in the early part of the war. Richmond became the nexus for much of this capitalist and nationalized expansion. Some sources list the South/CSA as the fourth-richest country in the world in 1860–61.

During the war, Southerners laid nearly 1,600 new miles of rail line, an impressive number—until compared to the 16,000 laid by the North. The South was home to the world's most renowned flour at Gallego flour works in Richmond, which exported prewar flour around the world to at least four continents and in 1865, at the end of the conflict, was still the world's largest single flour processor. The South/CSA built (or converted) twenty ironclad warships in the conflict, a fleet that might have conquered any European nation. The James River Squadron, with ironclads, kept Richmond free from naval incursion until the end of the war.

Richmond became a magnetic focal point for the collection and use of many of the South's natural resources. Copper initially came from Tennessee, coal later from Alabama and saltpeter (needed for the manufacture of gunpowder) from southwest Virginia and eastern Kentucky, but the loss of border territory quickly meant that alternatives had to be developed from previously "worked out" mines or had to rely on risky imports needing to run through the blockade. One reason the Confederates printed paper money and didn't mint silver, copper and gold coins (to any great extent) was the need for all precious metals (in the limited amounts even available) to go straight into the military-industrial complex or a strategic reserve needed to negotiate foreign transactions.

The decline in iron production in Virginia prior to the war (only sixteen furnaces in operation in 1860), combined with the early loss of much of Tennessee, meant that one company, Tredegar, had to pull much of the weight of the overall war effort from early on:

> *When the war's first shots were fired on Fort Sumter, Tredegar was the nation's third largest iron manufacturer, specializing in heavy ordnance and a complete line of railroad products including locomotives, freight cars, wheels, axles, spikes, and even iron bridges. In addition, they made steam engines for ships and sugar mills. The furnaces were supplied with pig iron carried by horse drawn canal boats plying the James River and Kanawha Canal. The first shot, incidentally, came from a 10-inch mortar manufactured at Tredegar.*[9]

Because the Union blockade increasingly stopped the regular flow of commerce from abroad, and products imported from the North were mostly not available (although there was soon a thriving black market for some products, like coffee), the fledgling globalization of antebellum Richmond was abruptly cut off but quickly turned into a centralized and hastily planned militarization of the infrastructure.

The Confederate Congress and bureaucracy reacted quickly and with as much energy as their resources allowed. One of the most impressive projects was not in Richmond—a powder works planned in July 1861 that ultimately would provide many hundreds of thousands of pounds of powder:

> *Erected in a mere eight months, the works comprised a two-mile-long series of castellated Gothic revival buildings, straddling the Augusta Canal, that were designed to efficiently convert sulfur, niter* [saltpeter], *and charcoal into finished powder. At peak production, the Confederate Powder Works was capable of producing as much as 6,000 pounds of gunpowder per day, and by the end of the war, more than 3 million pounds had been produced.*[10]

Sallie Brock Putnam reported that several "chemists" who were smoking while they were finding ways to make gunpowder in 1861 caused a terrible explosion. The Confederate authorities had no powder for muskets, so they had to start from scratch to learn how to make it and mined unusual sources of material (such as guano, used to make niter—potassium nitrate). The CSA created a gunpowder mill at Augusta, Georgia, in early 1862, but Richmond remained central to the bureaucracy and production of powder.

Richmond became the center of ammunition manufacture. The Ordnance Bureau started the manufacture of ammunition in buildings at the end of Seventh Street. It was decided to clear Brown's Island in the James River for increased production. By 1863, hundreds of young women and even girls were employed there. The need for ammunition was enormous—each major battle used millions of rounds of bullets and tens of thousands of rounds of artillery ammunition. The complex constructed about 250,000 small-arms cartridges per day, or about 1.2 million per week.

There was little training and no safety guidelines, making an accident inevitable. On Friday, March 13, 1863, in a wooden building one hundred feet by fifty feet in size, about sixty workers were engaged in their usual tasks. At the far end of the room, Irish-born nineteen-year-old Mary Ryan was working with friction primers, small tubes filled with an explosive chemical. Sometimes they stuck in the wooden block which held them, and becoming impatient, workers tapped the block on the table to loosen them. There was a lot of loose gunpowder about and combustible dust in the air. It could have happened to anyone, but it happened to one of her friction primers. The explosion naturally blew the roof off the building. Worse was the fire that accompanied the explosion. Some victims ran into the river, their clothes on fire. Lacking modern knowledge for burn treatment, those with severe cases likely suffered painfully in recovery or until they died. Not all the details are known, but about fifty people died from the explosion, with others being maimed and scarred by the burns they received. But the factory was rebuilt and production resumed. It hired two hundred girls, but they were required to be over the age of fifteen. No other explosion happened on the premises after that.

Shortages of every type defined and characterized Richmond throughout the period of the Civil War. Only Confederate money existed in abundance, which inversely caused a shortage of everything else. The Confederate Congress simply passed laws that kept increasing the amount of currency in circulation. It accepted this solution in order to meet payment obligations to soldiers so that the CSA could continue the war. More and more "greybacks" in circulation with fewer and fewer goods to purchase created the classic situation of inflation. The Union created "greenbacks" as its currency in 1861. Both sides realized that mobilizing armies would require a huge quantity of currency. Until 1861, all physical money was in the form of coins. Some banks issued their own currencies that they would redeem "on demand," presumably in gold or silver. But the Union required a currency accepted in every state, and the Confederacy had the same needs.

It has already been mentioned that Richmond became the central focal point of a fledgling Confederate navy. According to *Civil War Navy* magazine, the yard in Richmond was one of at least thirty-four major naval sites developed by the CSA during the war, although arguably Richmond became the most important, as the capital city was literally only miles from hostile forces at all times and the Union-occupied Norfolk early in the war.

The James River Squadron, which included ironclads manufactured by the Confederacy in Richmond, probably did more than anything besides Lee's Army of Northern Virginia to keep the Union forces away from the capital. The fleet ultimately consisted of almost several dozen vessels from small torpedo boats. The four ironclad warships represented the most powerful class of warships in the world at the time and were a major reason the city held out until the land armies failed. The ironclads were a manufacturing and engineering feat that even impressed Union authorities. John Coski reported their basic statistics as follows:

TABLE 2. JAMES RIVER SQUADRON IRONCLADS

NAME	LENGTH	GUNS	YEAR LAUNCHED
CSS *Richmond*	180 feet	4	1862
CSS *Fredericksburg*	188 feet	4	1863
CSS *Virginia II*	201 feet	4	1863
CSS *Texas*	217 feet	6	1864*

*never fully completed

On the eve of the Civil War, the Tredegar Iron Works in Richmond employed roughly eight hundred workers, composed of both African Americans (enslaved and free) and whites. The company had government contracts for ordnance and was the largest ironworks and foundry in the South. The architect of this capitalism success story was Joseph R. Anderson.

JOSEPH R. ANDERSON

Anderson was born in Fincastle, Virginia, in 1813 and later graduated fourth in his class at West Point. His engineering and organizational talents were recognized by the army, and he supervised projects like the construction of Fort Pulaski in Savannah, Georgia. In 1841, he joined the management of Tredegar (incorporated in 1837); in 1848, he bought the company outright. The company was a major factor (along with some other industries in Richmond) in the decision to relocate the Confederate capital from Montgomery, Alabama, to Richmond. Anderson served as brigadier general and was wounded during the Seven Days Battles. Shortly thereafter, he resigned and returned to full-time management of the company, which continued to expand throughout the war.

The federal government seized the factory complex when Richmond fell to Union forces. Before that, Anderson armed some of his factory workers to keep his complex from going up in flames when Confederate troops retreated out of the city. Anderson regained control of the company in 1867. He and some of his associates had shipped cotton out of the country before the war with the proviso that they receive payment to their London bank. Thus, he was able to repatriate $195,000 in 1865 to save the business. The business

View of Tredegar Iron Works as it appeared after being saved from the evacuation fire. *Library of Congress.*

continued to thrive, and Anderson remained perhaps the most prominent businessman in pre- and postwar Richmond, serving a second time in the Virginia House of Delegates and wielding great influence.

Iron drove everything, and the iron industry took a series of early blows when places like Clarksville, Tennessee, were captured and occupied by Union forces. A foundry there had already been producing a small number of cast artillery pieces and was lost for the duration of the war. Such events only placed more pressure on the industry of Richmond. Tredegar could sometimes only work at one-third of its capacity due to a shortage of pig iron:

> *Tredegar's owner, Joseph Anderson, remarked in a July 1862 letter (cited in Dew, 1966), "Everything must stop unless we go into the mountains and purchase and operate blast furnaces to make pig iron." Anderson, with financial help from the Confederate government, managed to acquire ten furnaces west of the Blue Ridge. Four of them—Cloverdale, Grace, Glenwood, and Columbia—were in blast when acquired. Five of them— Australia, Caroline, Catawba, Rebecca, and Jane—needed repairs, while*

Elizabeth Furnace was ultimately too near to Union Army activities and was not brought back on line. Anderson had to find competent managers, acquire teams and wagons for hauling ore and pig iron, and provide food for hundreds of furnace laborers who rebuilt stacks and replaced machinery at furnaces long out of blast.[11]

Railroads, five of which converged in or near Richmond, were iron-based—cars, locomotives and rails that the cars rode on were all produced with iron. Scrap drives somewhat analogous to what would happen during World War II were conducted to find any kind of useful iron.

The South produced rolling stock and locomotives before the war. One source states that the last engine built at Uriah Wells's Locomotive and Car Works in Petersburg was completed in 1861, eventually named "The South"; it worked for the Confederate cause throughout the war. It was also recorded that Tredegar in nearby Richmond competed with Wells in the prewar market selling locomotives and had established a national reputation for its engines. Wells ultimately manufactured some twenty engines, all of the 4-4-0 type and apparently all of them before the war (excepting "The South," which was finished right at the start of the conflict).

The great financial panic of 1857 had driven many Virginia locomotive manufacturers out of business just prior to the war. The Smith & Perkins Locomotive Works in Alexandria, Virginia, declared bankruptcy that year, for example. Burr and Ettinger had stopped in about 1855; Talbott and Brother Iron Works produced only a handful of engines. Tredegar also produced locomotives, roughly seventy of them before the war. By the start of the war, however, roughly less than 10 percent of Southern locomotives on rosters were "domestically produced," and their ability to continue to produce declined due to financial and other factors. It is hard to find any evidence that a single engine was produced in the South during the war, although the technology and ability still existed. Guns were needed more than engines.

The Confederate government did not build any monumental architecture in Richmond (no resources could be spared for that), but it did convert, improve, improvise and engage in some new construction for war purposes. The naval yard that eventually sprawled along both sides of the river, for example, involved new construction as well as conversion or use of existing structures. The Confederate Congress spent large sums of money supporting the Richmond war industry, and for the first part of the war, the economy surged.

Soon the labor market tightened, and the beginning of military conscription in 1862 signaled a crisis that would never be fully resolved. Some laborers in the tobacco sector quickly shifted to work in war-related jobs. Some agricultural slaves were rented by their owners to factories and businesses (this was the law) but lived independently and moved about. Women, young girls and boys began to find work. But it wasn't long before the shortage became critical, constricting economic growth. One result was a series of running battles between civilians, state authorities and the Confederate army over critical military exemptions. General Lee, famous on the battlefield, was stingy with off-the-battlefield exemptions, telling state authorities and others repeatedly that he needed every man at the front.

The labor shortage also affected the Confederate government's ability to capitalize on its grand plans to build a military-industrial infrastructure. Producing ironclads in Richmond, for example, was barely feasible with constrained timber resources and with the limited iron on hand, but once the labor shortage took full effect, it made completing them nearly impossible. They didn't finish the CSS *Texas*. The government constructed a huge powder works in Georgia (a truly impressive complex that was massive even for its day) but then couldn't repair or man the railroads necessary to transport powder where it needed to go.

In spite of shortages everywhere, and even allowing women to work as war clerks in some Confederate offices, officials drew a hard line about women serving in the military itself, although many women tried and some succeeded in doing so:

> *Going South.—Lt. Buford, otherwise Mrs. Alice Williams, the female "Lieutenant," who was in Castle Thunder for appearing in male apparel, goes South this morning to Atlanta, Ga. It is hardly probable that this brave but eccentric woman will be kept out of the fights in Mississippi.*[12]

A prisoner on Belle Isle turned out to be Mary Jane Johnson, who had joined the Sixteenth Maine in disguise to follow her lover, who thereafter died in battle. She was moved to Castle Thunder, and rather than work in a factory, it was anticipated that she would be sent north with the next batch of parolees.

Some Union prisoners were employed on a parolee basis, and some did work in prison on odd jobs that helped the war effort. Authorities hesitated at first to dip too deeply into that labor pool but quickly adjusted to the reality of "all hands on deck."

Chapter 9

SEVEN DAYS BATTLES

It is not what you look at that matters, it's what you see.
—Henry David Thoreau

Lincoln summoned George B. McClellan the morning after the defeat at Bull Run to take command of a new army made up of three-year enlistees that would come to be known as the Army of the Potomac. On July 26, McClellan found in his words "no army to command—only a mere collection of regiments cowering on the banks of the Potomac." No matter his other faults, McClellan forged the Army of the Potomac into a formidable force. He was, in the end, an excellent administrator and trainer of troops. Lincoln believed that the Confederate army and not the Confederate capital should be the objective of the Army of the Potomac, but he went along with McClellan's plan to capture Richmond. McClellan made a wide turn around the Confederate army on the strength of the U.S. Navy transports landing at Fort Monroe and moving up the Peninsula between the York and the James Rivers. Richmonders rightly feared the threat of a force of more than 100,000 marching toward Richmond. General Joseph E. Johnston commanded the Confederate army facing McClellan.

Lincoln wanted McClellan to attack Johnston's forces at Manassas in the spring of 1862. Johnston anticipated McClellan's plan and withdrew from the area to the Rappahannock River forty miles south. Lincoln was upset to find that the abandoned Confederate defenses were not as strong as McClellan feared. Jefferson Davis was upset with Johnston, who

General Joseph E. Johnston. *Library of Congress.*

abandoned a significant amount of supplies because they could not be transported down muddy roads with his troops. Both presidents were unhappy with their commanding generals. Nevertheless, the wheels were in motion for a major conflict.

In March 1862, while serving as the military adviser to Jefferson Davis, Robert E. Lee conceived of the idea to create a diversion in the Valley to keep Union general Irvin McDowell's troops from linking up with General McClellan's group already on the Peninsula threatening Richmond. Lee's strategy and the flawless execution by Confederate general Stonewall Jackson accomplished the purpose. On May 24, 1862, Abraham Lincoln ordered McDowell to abandon his orders to join McClellan and head to the Valley of Virginia to attack Jackson's rear. Both McClellan and McDowell objected to Lincoln's orders and said that the withdrawal of McDowell to the Valley played into the enemy's plan. But McDowell had no choice.

In early May 1862, Johnston evacuated Yorktown, and Union forces took this opportunity to take Norfolk. The Confederacy blew up everything of military value, including the *Virginia*. The Union navy took a five-ship flotilla up the James River to attack Richmond. But on May 15, the batteries at Drewry's Bluff, seven miles below Richmond, were able to stop the gunboats since the *Merrimac* could not raise its gun high enough to hit Confederate guns entrenched on the bluffs. Confederate officials had begun the orders to

Drewry's Bluff, Virginia. View of a Columbiad gun in Fort Darling on the James River. *Library of Congress.*

pack archives to leave the city but were relieved along with the citizens of the city when the Federals were stopped.

The Chickahominy River flows south and empties into the James River halfway down the Peninsula. In late May 1862, heavy rains turned the river into a raging torrent that split Union forces. Jefferson Davis prodded Johnston to launch an attack. Johnston, strengthened to seventy-five thousand men under his command by troops from North Carolina, planned an attack on May 31. The armies clashed at Seven Pines (referred to as "Fair Oaks" in Union dispatches because of a railway station), where a national cemetery exists today at the intersection of Nine Mile Road and Route 60 (Williamsburg Road). The Confederates had the upper hand until the Union commander, sixty-five-year-old Edwin "Bull" Sumner, known as the leather-lunged leader of the Second Corps, got his troops over bridges almost under water and at dusk began battle on June 1, 1862. General Johnston was wounded in the battle, and Jefferson Davis replaced him with Robert E. Lee. From then on, these troops became known as the Army of Northern

Chickahominy River. Military bridge built by the Fifteenth New York Volunteers under Colonel John McL. Murphy. *Library of Congress.*

Virginia. At this point, Union troops were six miles from Richmond. Lee retreated, realizing the futility of further fighting.

Of the success at Fair Oaks, McClellan said that "victory had no charm for me when purchased at such cost." Such a quote confirms McClellan's belief in the teachings of Jomini, who advised against throwing armies against each other in the field. McClellan would have preferred to have pushed the enemy back with his overwhelming mass of forces than with a pitched battle.

Pundits in the Richmond newspapers and McClellan made disparaging remarks about Lee. The Richmond *Examiner* called him "evacuating Lee." McClellan, in words that would have better described himself, said that Lee was "cautious and weak under grave responsibility...likely to be timid and irresolute in action." Many in the Confederacy thought that Lee was the wrong man for the job. Lee was fifty-five—too old, some thought. But Lee had a clear vision of an offensive-defensive strategy. Lee evacuated the area on June 1 and set about strengthening defensives around Richmond. Lee always believed in building defenses because it saved the lives of his men over and over throughout the war. He set his troops strengthening fortifications and trenches around Richmond, and for this his troops referred to him as "the king of spades." But he posted a part of his forces behind these fortifications so that he could attack McClellan's exposed right flank on the north side of the Chickahominy River. He spent most of the month reorganizing units just coming into his army.

Lee's inclination always focused on offense. He had about 90,000 soldiers compared to McClellan's 110,000-man Army of the Potomac. At this point, astute reconnaissance by twenty-nine-year-old Jeb Stuart's cavalry

Battery B, Second U.S. Artillery near Fair Oaks, Virginia, June 1862. *Library of Congress.*

discovered that McClellan's right flank was "in the air," which means it had no natural or man-made barriers to protect the Union flank at this point. The emergence of Lee was the primary factor in the events affecting Richmond from June 1862 to the end of the war.

Lee secretly brought Jackson's troops, about 25,000, down from the Valley to attack Union general Fitz John Porter's Fifth Corps, consisting of about 30,000 troops. The Seven Days Battles began on June 25, 1861, with a small attack by Union forces. Lee began a series of attacks on June 26—the second day of the Seven Days Battles. Tired of waiting for Jackson to arrive, A.P. Hill attacked in the late afternoon without the support of Jackson's troops at Mechanicsville, with heavy losses. Confederate casualties were 1,500, with only 360 Union casualties. The reason for the delay was Jackson and his men were weary from the long journey and the various roadblocks the Union army put in the way to slow the Confederates. We suggest Douglas Southall Freeman's discussion of these events in *Lee's Lieutenants: A Study in Command* for more detail and color. McClellan declared Mechanicsville a

Left: Fair Oaks, Virginia professor Thaddeus S. Lowe observing the battle from his balloon *Intrepid*. *Library of Congress*.

Below: Professor Lowe inflating his balloon *Intrepid* to reconnoiter the Battle of Fair Oaks. *Library of Congress*.

"complete victory" but failed to take the initiative. McClellan, convinced of the superior numbers of the Confederate troops, began what he labelled a "change of base" that, in effect, was a retreat and abandonment of the planned Siege of Richmond. While Mechanicsville had been a tactical defeat for the Confederacy, it turned into a strategic victory since it stopped the Union advance. Imagine if Grant had been in command of the Army of the Potomac in June 1861. McClellan ordered Porter to fall back about four miles to a more defensible position at Gaines's Mill.

General Sykes and staff near Richmond, June 1862. *Library of Congress.*

On June 27, at Gaines's Mill, Confederate forces attacked Porter's forces in halting, poorly coordinated movements all morning long on a hot day. A.P. Hill was to attack Porter's center, while Longstreet attacked the left flank and Jackson the right flank. But Jackson was again slow getting in place. Hill's men received the brunt of the carnage. Near sundown, Lee got all of his forces engaged in a coordinated attack. Finally, John Bell Hood—a tall, bearded Texan brigadier—pierced Porter's line. Union reinforcements prevented a rout. While Lee won the battle, the cost was extremely high. In six hours of fighting, the South suffered nine thousand casualties—as many as two days of fighting at Shiloh. The cost to defend Richmond was beyond high. Lee continued to define plans to pursue Union forces, but delays, poor coordination, shoddy staff work and simply timid leaders allowed the Union to take strong positions at Malvern Hill. Frontal assaults by Confederates resulted in severe carnage across Confederate units. Commanders under McClellan urged attacks, but McClellan was a man more defeated than his troops and commanders. Lee was lucky to face that kind of enemy.

Wagon train of Military Telegraph Corps. *Library of Congress.*

Parrott rifled guns of the First New York Battery, 1862. *Library of Congress.*

Lee planned to attack the flanks of the retreating Union divisions, but lack of coordination and the lethargy of Jackson's troops hampered Lee's plans. Some minor engagements took place at Garnett's and Golding's Farm on June 27 and 28. June 29 saw the next meaningful engagement when three Union divisions formed a rear guard to protect a field hospital and a huge wagon train moving south at Savage's Station. The Union army withdrew during the night, leaving the wounded with some surgeons to be taken prisoner.

The next day, on June 30, another of Lee's complicated plans for a concentric assault by seven divisions at the village of Glendale came apart. Rebel casualties were 3,500 to about half of that for Union forces. Again Stonewall Jackson failed in his command to support Hill and Longstreet.

On July 1, Union forces took up a very strong position three miles south of Glendale at Malvern Hill—150 feet high and flanked by ravines. Staff work was again uncoordinated, and attacks on the Union's entrenched positions allowed the Union to pulverize the attacking Confederates. Confederate casualties were 5,500 compared to about half of that for the Union side.

Savage Station. Headquarters of General George B. McClellan on the Richmond and York River Railroad. *Library of Congress.*

Savage Station. Virginia Union field hospital after Battle of Gaines's Mill, June 27, 1862. *Library of Congress.*

Recognizing the blow to the Confederate side in this battle, several Union generals wished to take the offensive and still take Richmond. But McClellan still insisted on retreating to Harrison's Landing. Lee realized the futility of continuing the conflict. The Army of Northern Virginia had suffered 20,000 killed or wounded, nearly a quarter of the army. The Union had lost half as many, although some accounts put its casualties as high as 16,000.

Family literally met family on the battlefield. Captain D.P. Conyngham of the Union Irish Brigade penned this account from Malvern Hill:

> *I had a Sergeant Driscoll, a brave man, and one of the best shots in the Brigade. When charging at Malvern Hill, a company was posted in a clump of trees, who kept up a fierce fire on us, and actually charged out on our advance. Their officer seemed to be a daring, reckless boy, and I said to Driscoll, "if that officer is not taken down, many of us will fall before we pass that clump." "Leave that to me," said Driscoll; so he raised his rifle, and the moment the officer exposed himself again bang went Driscoll, and over went the officer, his company at once breaking away. As we passed the place I said, "Driscoll, see if that officer is dead—he was a brave fellow."*

I stood looking on. Driscoll turned him over on his back. He opened his eyes for a moment, and faintly murmured "Father," and closed them forever. I will forever recollect the frantic grief of Driscoll; it was harrowing to witness. He was his son, who had gone South before the war. And what became of Driscoll afterwards? Well, we were ordered to charge, and I left him there; but, as we were closing in on the enemy, he rushed up, with his coat off, and, clutching his musket, charged right up at the enemy, calling on the men to follow. He soon fell, but jumped up again. We knew he was wounded. On he dashed, but he soon rolled over like a top. When we came up he was dead, riddled with bullets. [13]

News of the great battles taking place around Richmond spread quickly throughout the South. Mary Chesnut, then in South Carolina, recorded this in her diary on June 2:

A battle is said to be raging round Richmond. I am at the Prestons'. James Chesnut has gone to Richmond suddenly on business of the Military Department. It is always his luck to arrive in the nick of time and be present at a great battle. Wade Hampton shot in the foot, and Johnston Pettigrew killed. A telegram says Lee and Davis were both on the field: the enemy being repulsed. Telegraph operator said: "Madam, our men are fighting." "Of course, they are. What else is there for them to do now but fight?" "But, madam, the news is encouraging." Each army is burying its dead: that looks like a drawn battle. We haunt the bulletin-board.

Richmond received thousands of casualties and prisoners from this series of actions. None of these battlefields was far away. To be wounded and bouncing along in a wagon to Richmond would have been a horrific event. Thousands of Union soldiers were captured and sent to Richmond. Three bright spots in the Seven Days Battles for the Confederacy followed. First, the boost in morale for turning back such a significant threat raised the belief across the Confederacy and among some potential foreign allies that the Confederacy indeed could prevail. Second, significant resources abandoned by Union troops came into possession of the Confederate quartermaster. During the Seven Days Battles, Confederate ordnance officers gathered thirty thousand small arms and fifty cannons. Third, Lee grasped the need for a command structure that worked for him and would ensure that the mistakes of the Seven Days Battles would be avoided in the future.

The well-known bugle call "Taps" was composed at Harrison's Landing while McClellan's army waited to be transported back to Washington. General Daniel Butterfield wrote the twenty-four notes in a manual that he took with him on the Peninsula Campaign. One day, with the help of a brigade bugler, Oliver Wilcox Norton, whom he had summoned to his tent, they revised it to replace the bugle call the U.S. Army had been using to signal the end of the day.

Confederate Administration, Selected Biographies

Jefferson Davis, President

On February 6, 1865, Davis made Lee general-in-chief of all Confederate forces—too late. But it can also be argued that Lee was not enough of a strategic thinker for it to have made any difference. We will never know. About that time, Davis said, "If the Confederacy falls, there should be written on its tombstone: Died of a theory." The belief in the doctrine of states' rights weakened the CSA. Individual states, by recalling their military or refusing to pay what they owed, prevented the CSA from achieving all that it might have attained, or so Davis felt.

The famous military partnership between President Jefferson Davis and General Robert E. Lee started before the Seven Days Battles, but it is that momentous time that most people think of when they hear the two names mentioned together.

Davis was originally from Kentucky. He was born in Christian County in 1808, not far from where Abraham Lincoln would be born several months later. He was one of ten children in a military family and would successfully pursue his own military career, being described at West Point as "distinguished in his corps for manly bearing and high-toned and lofty character." He stopped his military career in 1835 to marry Sarah Taylor, daughter of Zachary Taylor, although she soon died of malaria. After that, Davis pursued business (a cotton plantation in Mississippi where he actually spent much of his life), entered politics (U.S. House of Representatives, U.S. senator, secretary of war) and remarried (Varina Howell in 1845, who would become first lady of the Confederacy).

Davis was far from beloved as president of the newly formed Confederacy. He was sometimes opinionated, stubborn and difficult, and he made his share of political enemies. He feuded regularly with the press. On the other hand, he was smart, competent and committed to his elected duties. He notoriously battled with certain generals and governors but almost always deferred to Lee. After the war, during a period of revisionist history, he was unfairly blamed for the South's ultimate defeat.

Davis was and remains an enigmatic figure in Civil War Richmond. He technically was not involved in direct city governance, but sometimes his policy agenda and leadership decisions meant that he was inevitably dragged into local politics. According to most accounts, he joined the efforts of Governor Letcher and Mayor Mayo attempting to stop the 1863 Bread Riot (and according to some accounts was mostly ignored and even scolded by some of the women).

The "White House of the Confederacy" was often used for public events, ranging from fundraisers to political events such as inaugurations. The citizens of Richmond often saw Jefferson walking around the capitol, and in spite of his idiosyncratic, argumentative personality, he was seen as accessible to the ordinary people. He once reportedly said, "Never be haughty to the humble or humble to the haughty."

White House of the Confederacy, 1201 East Clay Street. *Library of Congress.*

Others were not so kind. Stonewall Jackson, according to James I. Robertson, once said of Davis, "I saw no exhibition of that fire which I supposed him to possess." Another general said, "His authority is not sufficiently felt to correct existing evils and his manners are cold and repelling."[14]

Could anyone succeed facing what the Confederacy faced? Would the South have prevailed even if Lincoln had been president in Richmond? Davis copied the U.S. Constitution mostly but had no infrastructure in place that mimicked a viable nation. Everything had to be set up to operate and report quickly. Problems were solved as they arose. This made the Confederacy slow to coordinate railroads, industrial production and many other things that could have made the South more successful in the war. The verdict on Jefferson Davis may always be under deliberation. On June 10, 2020, protestors pulled down his statue on Monument Avenue. After the war, Davis was charged with treason, and later Horace Greeley reportedly paid part of his bail. His U.S. citizenship was restored in 1978.

To get a full picture of what happened for four years, a few short descriptions of key figures will help shed light on their importance with short summaries of the actions of key individuals.

Judah P. Benjamin, Secretary of State

Judah P. Benjamin was a U.S. senator from Louisiana before resigning to take up residence in Richmond. Jefferson Davis, who knew his abilities from their Senate days, appointed him attorney general of the Confederate States of America. But he had little to do and became secretary of war before finally finishing his Confederate career as secretary of state. He had a brilliant mind. He recognized early on that the belief that King Cotton would bring Britain and France to recognize the CSA would not work. Instead, he advocated by 1863 to use the sale of cotton to fund purchases of supplies for the army. His attempts to get foreign recognition for the Confederacy failed. President Davis's policy of complete embargo of cotton exports failed. Benjamin supported trading cotton with the North for bacon for the army in areas of the Western Theater. A great many families smuggled cotton through the lines in order to keep their families from starving. His brilliant mind was never utilized by President Davis in ways that could have made a difference in the outcome. He fled to Britain after the war and became a successful barrister in London.

Christopher G. Memminger, Secretary of the Treasury

Christopher G. Memminger believed that withholding cotton from world markets would bring Britain and France to the aid of the Confederacy. But it was a false belief held by many Southern leaders besides Davis and Memminger, who still lobbied hard to prevent Congress from passing laws embargoing the export of cotton. They did, in fact, encourage the shipment of cotton when possible. A Confederacy-wide policy would have benefited the South in regards to cotton. Memminger's biggest failure was to rely on the issuance of paper notes to finance the war.

The mindset of the Confederacy opposed taxation. According to Paul Escott, when Memminger first proposed meaningful taxation, the very wealthy men in Congress opposed the idea strongly. Thus, the Confederate Treasury printed paper money to pay its bills and wages of those in the army and employed by the government. The Union relied mostly on bonds and taxes to fund the government. From the start of the Confederacy in 1861 to January 1864, the supply of paper money increased elevenfold. Approximately 60 percent of the income for the Confederate government came from the issuance of paper money. Memminger resigned on July 1, 1864.

Alexander H. Stephens, Vice President

The remnants of Alexander H. Stephens's career consisted of jabs and criticisms directed at Jefferson Davis, who should have replaced Stephens. He said of Davis that the people should check his "fearful strides toward a

Residence of Alexander H. Stephens, vice president, CSA. *Library of Congress.*

centralized government with unlimited powers." His one job should have been to aid and support Davis, but he was not inclined to do that.

Josiah Gorgas, Chief of Ordnance

As chief of ordnance for the Confederate armies, Josiah Gorgas managed to provide the armies, against extremely long odds, with weapons and ammunition, despite the blockade and even hardly any munitions industry before the war began. During the Civil War, Fraser, Trenholm & Company, a British firm working in Charleston, acted as the overseas banker of the Confederate States of America, financing the supply of weaponry and essential goods in exchange for cotton, tobacco and turpentine. Gorgas relied on it to obtain munitions for the Confederacy.

In 1861, his task appeared hopeless. Gorgas, however, proved to be a genius at organization and improvisation. He created a Mining and Niter Bureau that found limestone caves containing saltpeter. The Ordnance Bureau built a huge gunpowder mill in Augusta, Georgia. Gorgas sent agents across the Confederacy to find stills for copper to make percussion caps, for example. They also requisitioned church bells and plantation bells for cannons. Lastly, they surveyed battlefields for gleaned lead to be remolded into bullets and collected guns to be repaired.

THE SIGNIFICANCE OF THE SEVEN DAYS

We believe that the impact of the Seven Days preserved Richmond from a similar assault up the Peninsula. It possibly knocked taking Richmond as an objective off the table. When Richmond fell, Grant continued to pursue Lee's army. Taking Richmond was not Grant's objective. It cemented Lee's reptation as the best hope of the Confederacy, although it came at a significant cost. The biggest command outcome was that Lee settled on his final command structure with what he learned during this time. He did not have a staff that was adequate enough to coordinate some of the complex things he was trying to put in motion before the Seven Days. This experience and his new command structure enabled Lee and the Army of Northern Virginia to achieve its greatest victories. However, it also meant that McClellan would never receive a top-level command post again, even though he won at Antietam. In a roundabout way, it opened the door for Grant to take over the Eastern Theater. McClellan and the Army of the Potomac squandered a number of opportunities to bring the war to an end much sooner. Some of McClellan's subordinates showed the vision and resolve to end the war but never got the chance.

Chapter 10

PRISONS AND HOSPITALS

With the first encounters, the clash of troops produced prisoners and patients sometimes in equal numbers. Neither side was prepared to deal with the number of wounded produced by military clashes because both sides believed the war would be over soon. Hospitals and prisons took over every available tobacco warehouse. Hospitals and prisons became the city's primary industries, employing thousands.

Prior to the outbreak of the war, a new kind of weapon became available to armies. In 1848, a French army officer, Claude-Etienne Minié, invented the Minié ball. Before the war, the army used a smoothbore musket that fired a smooth lead ball. It could not cover a very long distance. The shorter range of rifles early in the war meant that troops would engage in more frontal assaults resulting in more dire wounds. However, even after Confederate troops acquired better rifles, commanders still foolishly ordered frontal assaults on both sides. If a smooth lead ball hits a person, it breaks the skin and any bone that it came into contact with. The Minié ball had the shape of rockets shot to the moon—conical head and flat bottom. James Burton, an armorer working at the Harper's Ferry Armory, improved the bullet during the 1850s. His changes required a rifled gun barrel. At the start of the Civil War, both sides used mostly smoothbore muskets.

Northern industry geared up relatively quickly to produce rifles for the Minié ball. Jefferson Davis as secretary of war in 1855 converted the military to the .58-caliber Springfield rifled musket. The South could only produce limited quantities of this rifle. Instead, it relied on the rifles it could get through the blockade or captured Union weapons. But by 1863, nearly all soldiers on both sides carried these rifles. The Springfield rifle caused more injury when it struck a soldier. This became apparent in 1862 during the Seven Days Battles, as will be addressed later.

Confederates generally named battles by the name of the nearest town, whereas Union armies named battles by the nearest geographical marker. The first major battle of the war, the First Battle of Bull Run (the Union name), brought the horror of war into full view of both citizens and politicians from Washington, who rode out to see the battle, but also to the citizens of Richmond as the wounded came into the city. After hostilities ceased, the Union had suffered 2,708 casualties, including 481 killed, 1,011 wounded and 1,216 missing (presumed prisoners), while the Confederates had 1,982 casualties, with 387 killed, 1,582 wounded and 13 missing. With roughly 18,000 Southern troops engaged, that's more than 10 percent casualties. Little in the way of field hospitals had even been considered at that time.

At the beginning of the war, there was little thought given to ambulances or how to get wounded soldiers from the battlefield. At the First Battle of Bull Run, many wounded soldiers lay on the battleground for days. Field hospitals were usually a nearby church or large home. Sanitation did not even reach the level of afterthought. In short, they were dirty places more like slaughterhouses than what we expect today. Knowledge of disease and

First Battle of Bull Run, Virginia, July 21, 1861. *Library of Congress.*

Dead on battlefield at First Battle of Bull Run, 1861. *Library of Congress.*

First Battle of Bull Run, July 21, 1861. Union general McDowell and Confederate general Beauregard. *Library of Congress.*

sanitation were still in their infancy. Of the 620,000 soldiers (an astounding number even today) who died on both sides, most died from infection or diseases for which there was no cure. Illnesses like dysentery, typhoid fever, pneumonia, mumps, measles and tuberculosis spread among the poorly sanitized camps, killing men already weakened by fierce fighting and meager diet. The Union side did a better job of stepping up to the task and developing a system for effective ambulance and hospital services.

The wounded and dying were brought to Richmond mostly by train since roads would have been a hazardous ride in a wagon while wounded. The city administration and its citizens sprang into action from the beginning of the war. After the First Battle of Bull Run, Mayor Mayo called for a mass meeting at Capitol Square on July 22, 1861. One group formed to bring the wounded back to Richmond, and another group organized to establish facilities to care for the wounded. Every woman thought of herself as a nurse, and every house would become a miniature hospital. R.H. Dickinson, owner of the St. Charles Hotel at the corner of Main and Wall Streets, offered his establishment to serve as such. A citizen, Charles Bates, solicited cooks and nurses for a new hospital at the Second Market between Marshall and Broad

Confederate field hospital near Richmond, Virginia, April 1865. *Library of Congress.*

on Sixth Street. Within a month, about $8,000 had been raised to care for 1,336 patients. The city council provided plots at Oakwood Cemetery for those who died while being treated in the city. In this initial phase of the war, Sallie Brock Putnam commented that "almost every house in the city was a private hospital, and almost every woman a nurse."

In future battles, sometimes wounded prisoners from the Union side would be treated in Richmond facilities. Plus, there were a lot of family members traveling to Richmond to care for sons and fathers or to take them home for rest. It must have been a very chaotic situation for weeks after each battle. But Richmonders rose to the challenge, according to accounts from those days.

Many other activities sprang up to assist in this effort. The Richmond Young Men's Christian Association (YMCA) collected and distributed articles for patients. The women of St. James Episcopal Church secured the home of Judge John Robertson to serve as a hospital whose administrator was the very able Sally Louisa Tompkins. Her family name appears in the name of the Tompkins-McCaw Library of Virginia Commonwealth University's Medical Campus, not only for her work but also for the work of later generations of the Tompkins family. She was the remarkable woman who ran the Robertson Hospital, which became known for its astonishing record of low mortality rates. Others opened a "Soldiers Rest" in a school building on Clay Street. Performers and others put on shows to benefit the wounded and those who cared for the wounded. Volunteers from other Confederate states organized hospitals devoted to the care of soldiers from their state.

The Confederate government operated the largest medical facilities. After Bull Run, Confederate surgeon general S.P. Moore assigned patients to the newly constructed Alms House, which was henceforth called General Hospital No. 1. Moore's staff ultimately created and staffed twenty-eight general hospitals. Confederate citizens of Richmond held soldiers in high regard not just because of their value as soldiers but also because they represented the causes and ideals that the CSA stood for in a tangible way. Citizens sacrificed for soldiers as much as they could.

One effort of Dr. Moore's stood out head and shoulders above all the others. One of Dr. Moore's colleagues, Dr. William Brown McCaw (1823–1906), asked if he could convert some newly constructed barracks on Chimborazo Hill into a military hospital in the fall of 1861. He was another member of the Tompkins and McCaw families for whom the Virginia Commonwealth University Health Sciences library (Tompkins-McCaw Library) is named. McCaw secured for the fledgling hospital the status of

Envelope with message: "Lovely woman. We will take care of the brave soldiers who have fought our battles." *Library of Congress.*

Above: Chimborazo Hospital National Monument, National Park Service. *Photo by Derek Kannemeyer.*

Right: Plaque marking the spot of Florida hospital. *Photo by Derek Kannemeyer.*

THE FLORIDA HOSPITAL
OF RICHMOND, VIRGINIA

THIS BUILDING WAS PART OF THE FLORIDA HOSPITAL, ALSO CALLED THE GLOBE
HOSPITAL, AND GENERAL HOSPITAL #11, DURING THE WAR BETWEEN THE STATES.
FORMERLY IT HAD BEEN THE TOBACCO FACTORY OF JAMES H. GRANT, BUILT IN 1852.

IT HAD BEEN PURCHASED BY A DELEGATION FROM FLORIDA INCLUDING MARTHA REID,
THE WIDOW OF THE 4TH TERRITORIAL GOVERNOR OF FLORIDA. DR. THOMAS PALMER
WAS THE SURGEON, AND MARTHA REID WAS THE MATRON. ON OCTOBER 18, 1863, THE
RICHMOND ENQUIRER STATED THE LOW MORTALITY STATISTICS (ABOUT 4.8%) WERE
DUE TO THE SURGEONS, "AND ALSO TO THE CARE AND ATTENTION OF THE GENTLE,
ENERGETIC AND DEVOTED MATRON, MRS. EX-GOVERNOR REID, OF FLORIDA."

ERECTED NOVEMBER 2012
FOR THE SESQUICENTENNIAL OF THE WAR
IN MEMORY OF OUR NAMESAKE, MARY MARTHA REID
BY THE MARTHA REID CHAPTER 19, UDC, JACKSONVILLE, FLORIDA
DIANNE DRAKE BOREN, PRESIDENT

an independent army post. This designation gave him more freedom to run the hospital that ultimately treated seventy-six thousand patients during the war. It was the largest military hospital before World War I. It was a sprawling complex of 150 buildings and tents across Chimborazo Hill. He ran a bakery that produced up to ten thousand loaves of bread per day. The hospital had cows and goats that grazed at Tree Hill Farm, owned by a

1860 almshouse/CSA hospital/CSA barracks. Today apartments. *Photo by Misti Nolen.*

patriotic Southerner. It ran so efficiently that it could lend the Confederate Treasury money, resulting in a debt of $300,000 at the end of the war, a very large sum in those days. It operated a canalboat that brought supplies from Lynchburg. All of these measures and efficiencies resulted in a death rate of less than 10 percent.

To run all of the hospitals and provide all the care required over months took thousands and thousands of people. Of course, there were surgeons, doctors and nurses present in these facilities. Ads appeared in the papers looking for cooks, laundry workers, sanitation staff, administrators, bookkeepers, purchasing personnel and inventory clerks. The composition of each of these pools was diverse. Nurses, for instance, were men and women, many free and possibly some slaves hired out to the government. The categories and roles that existed before the war got turned upside down during the conflict. These impacts plus emancipation would begin to change Southern society and ultimately politics in Richmond and Virginia.

Richmond's wartime hospitals grew into a world of their own. It was inevitable that Richmond as the new Confederate national capital (a nation that included eleven states plus rump governments in Kentucky and Missouri) would become a center of army medical resources and organization. There were as many as fifty or more hospitals functioning in the city at any given time during the war. Some hospitals were housed in existing buildings (such as tobacco warehouses); some were built as brand-new construction (such as Chimborazo, the biggest hospital complex for either side, with seven thousand beds during the war); and some were temporarily maintained in private homes or businesses (such as General Hospital No. 6, which took over a clothing store on Main Street). There were often between ten to fifteen thousand wounded soldiers in these hospitals during peak battle seasons. Richmond newspapers list various hospitals opening and closing. Usage and demand fluctuated all the time, and as some hospitals got larger, it made sense to close others. (For a fuller account, see Rebecca Barbour Calcutt's book *Richmond's Wartime Hospitals*.)

More than 110,000 patients were treated in the first year plus of the war in Richmond. The following table will give the reader a sense of how busy the medical complex became during the war:

TABLE 3. NUMBER OF MILITARY HOSPITALS IN THE RICHMOND AREA DURING THE WAR

MONTH/YEAR	NUMBER OF HOSPITALS
April 1861	5
December 1861	16
April 1862	20
September 1862	50
October 1864	20

Source: Partially derived from Calcutt, *Richmond's Wartime Hospitals*.

Over the course of the war, at least eighty-five separate hospitals have been documented. Part of the reason for the large number was a practical one—it was difficult to maintain large hospitals without preexisting spaces suited to the purpose—but another reason related to a form of Southern identity with home states that might seem strange to today's readers. Hospitals were mostly organized by state, and wounded soldiers kept together as an ad hoc group.

Most of the larger hospitals all had a "dead house," a temporary place (a shed, a lean-to, another nearby building) to cover and hold bodies of the deceased until they could be transported somewhere else for burial. During times of sickness or great battles, the dead houses filled to overflowing. In the second half of the war, the bodies were stored nude or in undergarments so the uniforms could be washed, mended and used again.

Richmonders, for better or worse, began to identify with their city metaphorically as one large medical center. As healthy men were conscripted, hospitals increasingly employed female volunteers, free or enslaved African Americans and even children for some tasks. Medical support became the main occupation besides survival for many.

As an example of the elaborate network soon created, the hospital list from the Richmond *Dispatch* of June 4, 1862, is reproduced here:

TABLE 4. HOSPITAL DIRECTORY

The following is a list of the different hospitals and their locations in the city.

Army Hospitals (16)
Banner Hospital, corner of Franklin and Nineteenth Streets
Byrd Island Hospital, southern termination of Ninth Street, near the river
Camp Winder Hospital, western suburbs of the city
Chimborazo Hospital, on the hill overlooking Rockett's
First Alabama Hospital, Broad Street, between Twenty-Fourth and Twenty-Fifth Streets
First Georgia Hospital, Twenty-First Street, between Main and Cary
General Hospital, northern terminus of Second Street
Globe Hospital, on Nineteenth Street, between Main and Franklin
Greaner's Hospital, Twenty-First Street, between Main and Franklin Streets
Louisiana Hospital (formerly Baptist College,) western termination of Broad Street
Maryland Hospital, corner of Cary and Twenty-Fifth Streets
Royster's Hospital, on Twenty-Fifth Street, between Main and Franklin Streets
Second Alabama Hospital, corner of Franklin and Twenty-Fifth Streets
Second Georgia Hospital, Twentieth Street, between Main and Franklin
South Carolina Hospital, Manchester (approached by Mayo's bridge, end of Fourteenth Street)
Third Georgia Hospital, corner of Franklin and Twenty-Fourth Streets

Private Hospitals (6)
Baptist Church Hospital, Fourth Street, between Leigh and Duval
Bellevue Hospital, Broad Street, Church Hill

College Hospital, corner of Marshall and Eleventh Streets
Robertson's Hospital, corner of Main and Third Streets
Sailors' Home, corner of Clay and Henry Streets
St. Francis D'Sale, Brooke Avenue, near Bacon Quarter Branch

Hospitals Recently Opened/Emergency Hospitals (13)
Breeden & Fox's store, corner Broad and Fourth Streets
Crew's (factory) Hospital, corner of Cary and Twenty-First Streets
Hospital tents erected at Howard's Grove
Kent, Paine & Co.'s Hospital, Main, between Eleventh and Twelfth Streets
Keen, Baldwin & Co.'s Hospital, Main, below Governor Street
Liggon and Howard's (factory) Hospitals, Main Street, between Twenty-Fifth and Masonic Hall, Franklin, between Eighteenth and Nineteenth Streets
Mayo's and Dibrell's warehouses and the Danville workshops, in Manchester, would be used as hospital as soon as the necessary arrangements could be made
Richardson & Co.'s store, Main Street, below Fourteenth
Ross' (factory) Hospital, opposite Richardson & Co.'s store
Seabrook's Warehouse, corner of Grace and Eighteenth Streets
Spotswood Hospital, under Spotswood Hotel
St. Charles Hotel, corner of Main and Wall Streets (Twenty-Sixth Street)

The system was taxed to the breaking point the first year of the war, with the Richmond *Examiner* reporting in 1862 that more than 110,000 patients had been treated in the hospitals of Richmond (and Petersburg). Interestingly, the report also noted that "the smallest percentage of deaths has occurred in hospitals superintended by ladies."

A noteworthy detail involves the selfless work of Catholic nuns in roles as nurses on both sides (and in Richmond) during the war:

> *A key group of women nurses in the Civil War included the Daughters of Charity—established in America by Elizabeth Ann Seton in Emmitsburg, Maryland, in 1809. This congregation was founded in 1633 in France by Saints Vincent de Paul and Louise de Marillac to work among the sick poor. De Paul's 1655 Common Rules of the Congregation of the Mission stipulated that in any war, the sisters were not to prefer one side or the other…the Daughters of Charity worked in both Northern and Southern*

Moore Hospital (Confederate), Main Street, Richmond, Virginia, April 1865. *Library of Congress.*

hospitals. In sum, more than 600 Catholic sisters worked as nurses during the war, but the largest number were by far the Daughters of Charity: 232 nursed at one time or another in general hospitals, in field hospitals, and on hospital ships.[15]

Another interesting footnote in the history of psychiatry and mental health–related disability is that Confederate authorities set up a hospital (General Hospital No. 13) to deal specifically with psychological disorders, such as depression, what is now called PTSD and anxiety. "Also called the Lunatic Hospital," according to Stephen Ash, "it treated government wards suffering from mental disorders." Although a similar institute was set up on the Union side, these efforts were more than one hundred years ahead of their time in terms of the science and medical technique. Nevertheless, they represent the enormity of the commitment to the war effort.

Many innovations came about as a need of necessity. Confederate authorities in Richmond, for example, were some of the first in the world to modify rail cars into special ambulance train cars to move the wounded more effectively. Changes to treatment of soldiers made in the Civil War remained common practice through the beginning of World War II.

PRISONERS OF WAR

On a combined scale, prisoners of war amounted to at least 215,000 Confederates captured by the North, with at least 195,000 Union troops captured by the CSA. About 56,000 prisoners died in captivity, according to the National Park Service, or slightly less than 14 percent of the total combined prison population. Prisoner deaths represented 9 to 10 percent of the total estimated deaths of 750,000 during the Civil War. The suffering was roughly equal on both sides, as neither side was prepared to deal with this many prisoners over a period of time. Naturally, atrocities grew from the conditions each had little control over. Andersonville Prison in Georgia remains marginally the worst Southern prison. Its commandant, Henry Wirz, was the only Confederate executed for war crimes. Richmond prisons were undoubtedly bleak, but there never existed a policy to harm any prisoner. When the South struggled to feed its armies, prison supplies were the first to be curtailed.

Richmond operated at least twenty-five separate POW camps or prisons during the Civil War. Not all were active at the same time, and it was common for prisoners to be shuffled from one to another as other arrangements were made and overall numbers grew. No records state how many spent short or long amounts of time in Richmond. Another undocumented statistic is how likely it was for a soldier to be captured. It doesn't matter, however, as the result of going to either side's prisons was potentially devastating. Of the fifty-six thousand who died in captivity, more were Confederate than Union. Neither side had a policy aimed at prisoner reduction. There was no preparation for the level of prisoner intake that occurred. Belle Isle at its peak population, for example, had more than ten thousand Union inmates by itself, housed in tents as much as available, otherwise they lived in the open no matter the season. Conditions on both sides were terrible.

RICHMOND PRISONS

Belle Isle, a fifty-four-acre island in the middle of James River just above the fall line in Richmond, was home to a small village and ironworks before the war. During the war, it served a completely different purpose. Starting in 1862, the Confederate authorities began to use it as a POW camp for Union prisoners. There were no reasonable facilities on the island to accommodate

Prison camp at Belle Isle for Union enlisted soldiers. *Library of Congress.*

the roughly thirty thousand soldiers who were processed through the camp over the course of several years, and numbers vary about those who died in captivity, although the number is generally regarded as at least one thousand or more men. Prisoners lived outside, sometimes digging small dugouts in the sand as a partial shelter. Some lucky prisoners were issued Sibley tents, in which multiple men crowded together. During a rainstorm, the island could literally become a morass of mud, sand, silt and water, and the prisoners—even those with tents—had little protection.

The island could only be reached by bridge, and especially during high water it was surrounded by Class IV ("man-killer") rapids. Authorities considered this an advantage, as there were no walls, no "dead zone," no wire obstacles. It only took a few foolish men to try swimming away to dispel any notion that escape was likely by the water route. There are accounts, probably not apocryphal, of Confederate guards betting on swimmers who took the dive in. There are a few accounts of men actually surviving the attempt. When men from Belle Isle reached Baltimore and points northward after prisoner exchange, President Lincoln and others were appalled by their condition. To this day, the natural beauty and fascinating archaeology of the island are cast in the shadow of its wartime years. Each side had prison horror stories.

Libby Prison was established in a large warehouse and was home to many unhappy prisoners (almost all officers), who knew all too well that it was not designed for its purpose. It belonged to Luther Libby before the war. The Confederacy, in its haste to house prisoners, commandeered the building. There was not even time to remove the sign, so that's how it got its name. Prisoners were housed on the second and third floors. The windows were open holes in the walls covered by wooden bars, which made it very

Above: Libby Prison, Union prisoners, showing officers. *Library of Congress.*

Opposite: Libby Prison (converted tobacco warehouse), for Union officers, April 1865. *Library of Congress.*

hot in the summer and very cold in the winter. Only officers ended up being housed here. Enlisted men went to Belle Isle. No policy existed that would make life hard or dangerous at Libby, but because of shortages and intermittent cruelty by guards and overseers, many did suffer and die there. Prisoners could buy extra food and cook it in the prison. Lieutenant David Todd, Mary Todd Lincoln's half brother, was briefly commandant of Libby Prison. He was said to have been overly cruel to prisoners. All five of Mary Todd Lincoln's brothers served in Confederate armies. After the war, Libby Prison was dismantled to be displayed at the Chicago World's Fair but was never returned to Richmond.

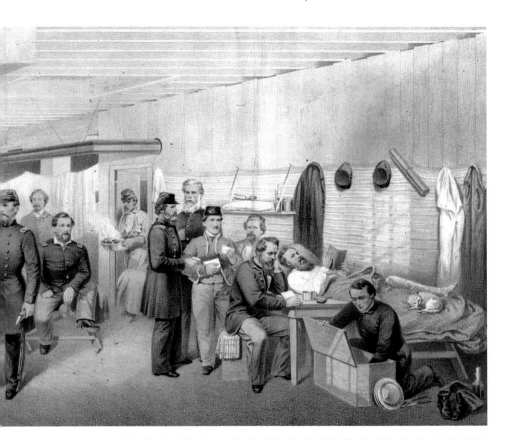

RAMPING UP PRISON INFRASTRUCTURE

Like the need for hospitals, the need to equip POW camps became manifest very quickly in the war. Richmond's proximity to Washington, D.C., (less than one hundred miles) meant that the major battlefields of the war were all generally within a one-hundred-mile radius or so of Richmond, and prisoners naturally collected there, even when they were eventually shipped to North Carolina or camps farther south. There's no exact number, but it's likely that at least 100,000 Union prisoners passed through or were detained for some time in Richmond.

The four most infamous Richmond Civil War POW camps or prisons probably include Libby Prison, which served as headquarters for CSA POW operations and ultimately housed mainly Union officers (located at Cary and Canal); Castle Thunder, which hosted more than 1,400 political prisoners, dissenters and deserters (located on the northern side of Cary between Seventeenth and Eighteenth); the less well-known Castle Lightning, which housed those "criminally accused Confederate soldiers and civilians" from around the region and even the nation (located at the corner of Sixth and Cary according to papers; note that the NPS locates it "across the street from Castle Thunder"); and Belle Isle, the very notorious outdoor prison camp on a James River island surrounded by deadly rapids.

Authorities also made use of guard dogs, including a nearly two-hundred-pound Russian bloodhound named "Hero" brought from Russia just before the war by a "Southern gentleman" to be used in arena sports. The dog worked as a guard dog at both Libby Prison and Castle Thunder. Hero was an enormous dog that put fear into anyone who even looked at him. Recall that most men then were not as large as the average man today and that prisoners were even smaller since they most likely lost weight in prison. Hero was seized by CSA prison authorities and reportedly engaged in bear fights.

TABLE 5. PRISONS IN CIVIL WAR RICHMOND

Atkinson's Factory	City Jail
Barrett's Factory	Crew & Pemberton's Warehouse*
Belle Isle	Franklin Street Guard House
"The Cage"	General Hospital No. 21*
Castle Godwin	General Hospital No. 22*
Castle Lightning	Grant's Factory*
Castle Thunder	Harwood's Factory*

Castle Thunder (converted tobacco warehouse). *Library of Congress.*

A Russian bloodhound guarded Union prisoners at Libby Prison and Castle Thunder. *Library of Congress.*

Henrico County Jail
Libby Prison
Liggon's Prison*
"Officer's Prison on 18th Street"
Prison Depot*
"Prison opposite Castle Thunder"

Ross Factory Hospital*
Scott's Factory Prison
Second Alabama Hospital*
Smith Factory Prison
State Penitentiary

*indicates a facility that served as both a prison and a hospital during periods of the war

Source: civilwarrichmond.com

Maintaining an efficient and humane system was sometimes beyond the scope of officials' abilities or the resources at hand. In early 1862, the Richmond *Enquirer* reported that Union prisoners temporarily housed in Atkinson's Factory "destroyed machinery and tobacco in their prison" (January 14). On October 2 of the same year, the Richmond *Dispatch* reported that the "city jail is being repaired after being damaged by a prisoner; appeal for a new jail." The city jail was used as a POW overflow. As Confederate authorities knew well by 1862, taking care of POWs was almost as involved as caring for an active army in the field.

GENERAL SAMUEL WINDER

Confederate general Samuel Winder was provost marshal for Richmond between 1862 and 1864 and Confederate commissary of prisons until his death in February 1865 from a heart attack. Richmonders would forever remember him for the former role. This duty included, according to Encyclopedia Virginia, "Dealing with rampant prostitution, gambling, drinking, and speculation, as well as arresting the numerous deserters and spies who lurked around the city." It was a thankless job from just about every vantage point, and he became one of the least popular figures in town.

In reality, it was a nearly impossible job. New recruits came to Richmond, and there were few or no uniforms to issue them. Winder's staff took uniforms from dead soldiers and "refurbished" them. Superstitious soldiers didn't want to wear them. The citizens protested when he implemented price controls on food to try to control rampant inflation. He reorganized his staff in late 1862 and things got somewhat better, but wartime anecdotes and complaints about Winder dot the records.

Winder was most notorious for his oversight of Richmond prisons and eventually other Confederate prisons and POW camps. His death before the end of the war probably saved him from greater ignominy and blame, as sites like Andersonville revealed to the North (and even people in the Confederacy) how terrible conditions actually were in camps. Winder had a tremendous influence on events in the city during the war but is generally not remembered fondly.

PRISONER EXCHANGE

During the first few years of the war, prisoner exchange helped to manage prison populations. The way it worked was that a prisoner would be paroled. He promised not to fight again until his name was "exchanged" for a similar man on the other side. Then both of them could rejoin their units. While awaiting exchange, prisoners were confined to permanent camps. The exchange system broke down in mid-1863 when the Confederacy refused to treat captured Black prisoners as equal to white prisoners. The prison populations on both sides then soared.

Part of Union general U.S. Grant's "total war," or war of attrition, was to end prisoner exchanges, which he rightly understood were an inherently favorable tradeoff for the Confederates, who were exhausting their pools for manpower. The Union could absorb the losses in prisoners. Of course, Grant had to know that there would be a human toll to this, especially as evidence mounted that the Confederate authorities could not feed their own army, let alone care adequately for Union prisoners. Grant made the calculation, and as a result, Richmond went from closing some POW facilities in late 1863 and early 1864 to reopening them again out of necessity. As Grant intended, this stretched the fragile food and manpower situation to the breaking point.

Prisoners did sometimes escape from Richmond. Confederate authority basically extended to the picket lines of the Army of Northern Virginia, and if a man could get ten miles outside Richmond, he stood a better than favorable chance of making it to Union lines, keeping to woods and fields and avoiding sporadic patrols. With that said, Southerners did have experience with runaway slaves and sometimes used dogs, hastily formed posses and an informant network to track down escapees.

Chapter 11

UNIONISTS AND SPIES

Not everyone in Richmond supported secession, which was no surprise. After the election of Lincoln, not every state desired to secede immediately, but seven states did secede. However, they could not possibly challenge the Union without the resources of the upper South. Edmund Ruffin, a Virginian known as a hot-blooded secessionist, urged an attack on Fort Sumter. He wrote, "The shedding of blood will serve to change many voters in the hesitating states, from the submission or procrastinating ranks, to the zealous for immediate secession." After the attack on Fort Sumter by South Carolina militia and the surrender by the Union garrison on April 14, 1861, howls for war arose widely in the North. Lincoln issued a proclamation calling for seventy-five thousand militiamen into national service for ninety days to put down what he called an insurrection in the South.

The line in Virginia and hence Richmond was clearly drawn. People had to decide where they stood—for or against secession. The Virginia Secession Convention met in Richmond and leaned toward staying in the Union. Governor Letcher favored remaining in the Union along with a majority of Virginians, who at that point consisted of the present-day states of Virginia and West Virginia. Secessionists rallied sentiment for separation from the Union. Brendan Wolfe, in the Encyclopedia Virginia, noted, "Most white Virginians considered secession and slavery to be separate concerns, and indeed Virginia's Protestant churches opposed secession and supported slavery with the same moral certainty, at least until the war's first shots were fired." Once Virginia seceded, many struggled with the moral dilemma of loving their home but being opposed to secession and slavery or both. Secession put some people to the test. Most of those who enlisted in the CSA armed services did not own slaves.

A few people, such as Elizabeth Van Lew, and some religious denominations had long opposed slavery. Others who did not support the Confederate cause still saw the benefits of slavery. Pro-union support did not fall into neat categories. The *Dispatch* on March 6, 1862, reported, "The following parties have been arrested for supposed 'Union' proclivities since our last report: John Bennett, of Norfolk; Solomon Fenton, Jr., Memphis; Ebenezer Halleck, grocer, Main street; Rev. A. Bosserman, of Baltimore, Pastor of First Independent Christian Church, Mayo street.'" Newspapers from the war period have many such entries. Three days earlier, the *Dispatch* reported, "Mr. [John M.] Botts, of course, was well known to be opposed to the Southern movement; but his last publication on the subject, nearly a year ago, expressed his disapproval of the course of the President of the United States in bringing on the war, and his opinion that the South never could be subjugated. It was hoped that this fixed his position, and that he was Virginian enough at least to take no part against us." He and others were sent to Castle Godwin, "the new brick building on the extension of Fifteenth street, on the right-hand side, beyond the auction house of Messrs. Dickinson & Hill." The paper seemed to say it was acceptable to disagree but drew the line at taking actions against your friends and neighbors. But the message behind these publications was clear: someone is watching you, and your actions will be known to all.

A correspondent of the *New York Herald* ended up in Libby Prison and published an article in his paper on May 9, 1863. Northern papers were read all over the South when they could be obtained through exchange or on dead soldiers or in abandoned camps. One excerpt from the report is particularly germane to the perceptions of Unionists and how the reporter, J.H. Vosburg, felt about the state of the Confederacy. He wrote of conversations he picked up about Union sentiment:

Accounts from all portions of the confederacy were of rapidly approaching starvation, of general disaffection among the people, and of returning Union sentiment. In Georgia are some two thousand in the mountains who have so far successfully resisted the conscription, defeating a force sent to take them. In many places in the South our prisoners found Union people, who, in some cases, clandestinely offered them money. In nearly all the Southern jails are individuals confined and treated with great cruelty on the plea that they were still entertaining Union sentiments. In Knoxville particularly the Union sentiment predominates, and here citizen prisoners are treated with most atrocious severity.

While union sentiment was widespread, it may not have been very deep. On August 8, 1861, the Confederate Congress passed an Alien Enemies Act that required males, but not females, over age of fourteen who were not citizens of a Confederate state to swear an oath of allegiance to the CSA. If a person refused to take the oath, they would be deported to the Union. On August 30, the Confederate Congress, coming under pressure from not being harsh enough, strengthened the act by confiscating the property of those found disloyal.

ELIZABETH VAN LEW

In her book on Elizabeth Van Lew, *Southern Lady, Yankee Spy*, Elizabeth Varon noted, "But secession illustrated just how far slavery's partisans were willing to go to maintain their power." Once the war began, there was no room for abolitionists or those not supporting the CSA. Van Lew on visiting the troop training at Camp Lee said, in her journal, that she found them to be "of the very humblest class and deplorably ignorant." Everyone stood as one for the Confederacy once Virginia seceded and Richmond became the capital—this life, this war. Varon showed that Unionists stepped up to do what they could for Union soldiers captured at the First Battle of Bull Run. "'The entire stock of lint and bandages' for wounded Union soldiers from Manassas, prisoner William Harris wrote, was 'furnished by the Unionists of Richmond.'" Elizabeth Van Lew and her mother went to the prison shortly after the battle and were allowed to give Union soldiers what Van Lew said was "a little chicken soup and cornmeal gruel."

She managed to aid prisoners by pretending to be a loyal Southern lady doing Christian work aiding those most in need. She is known

Elizabeth Van Lew (1818–1900). *UVA Library.*

Elizabeth Van Lew mansion, front. *Library of Congress.*

to have bribed soldiers. The Van Lews offered to board Captain George C. Gibbs, head of the tobacco factory complex, along with his family in the Van Lew mansion. How could anyone suspect them of disloyalty after that? On January 23, 1862, Van Lew was prohibited from taking food to wounded Union prisoners. She fought back by writing letters to important people in the CSA. Ultimately, she received permission to resume her work with Union prisoners.

On March 1, 1862, Jefferson Davis suspended the writ of habeas corpus. He gave the job of enforcing martial law to General Winder and appointed him provost marshal general with the intention of ridding Richmond of spies and traitors. On March 2, his men arrested John Minor Botts. The Richmond *Enquirer* reported on March 4, "Mr. Botts was carried in a buggy to the private jail of McDaniel's on Franklin street, near Sixteenth, where he now remains." It also reported the arrest of Franklin Stearns, a known Union sympathizer who owned a distillery. The newspaper account noted, "When captured he remarked 'I suppose you take me because I am a Union man.' The officers replied that that was the reason, and added that they intended to arrest all of the same stripe in the city of Richmond, to which Mr. Stearns

Elizabeth Van Lew mansion, rear. *Library of Congress.*

responded, 'well, you'll have your hands full.'" Botts spent eight weeks in solitary confinement. He was released after promising not to publish any more incendiary letters and, in January 1863, moved to a plantation he had won gambling in Culpeper County.

Botts had promised that he would move away from Richmond to ensure his pardon. Stearns was confined to house arrest at his distillery, where his family could care for him. When you compare these actions by the CSA to the potential harm that could possibly have befallen them, we have to say that at least there were no summary executions. These were men known by many in the city, possibly friends of those who had to carry out these orders. It could have been so much worse. Compare the actions of the CSA to reprisals in the 1930s in Nazi Germany and Stalinist Russia to those suspected of disloyalty.

Botts, Van Lew and Stearns are all buried at Shockoe Hill Cemetery. Botts's epitaph reads, "I know no North, no South, no East, no West. I know only my Country, my whole Country, and nothing but my Country."

Van Lew in caring for Union wounded received support from those who if not supporters of the Union were at least sympathetic to the suffering

Elizabeth Van Lew grave at Shockoe Hill Cemetery. *Wikimedia Commons.*

of these prisoners. Reverend Thomas Moore of First Presbyterian Church (from 1847 to 1868) succeeded in obtaining access not only to Libby but also Castle Thunder, where Van Lew was prohibited. She donated money that the reverend distributed to prisoners, who could then buy food. Prisoners at Libby were allowed to buy extra food and cook it on their own.

There are fabulous stories of courage in aiding prisoners. For example, Erasmus Ross, nephew of Franklin Stearns, obtained the position of clerk at Libby Prison, responsible for keeping track of prisoners by roll call. Ross put up an at times elaborate subterfuge of anti-Union bravado to aid prisoners. Union captain William H. Lounsbury related how Ross threatened him and took him to a prison office. Varon recalled the story as follows:

> *As soon as the pair were in the office, Ross wordlessly directed Lounsbury to a Confederate uniform hidden behind a counter, which the Yankee prisoner hastily donned. Lounsbury then walked out the door and across the street to a vacant lot, only to be intercepted by an emissary from Van Lew: "…a colored man stepped out and said, 'Come with me, sah, I know who you is,' and he took me to Miss Van Lew's house on Church Hill."*

Her house provided a safe way station beyond Confederate lines. Slowly, Unionists across Richmond created an underground network to assist many getting out of Richmond to Union lines. This network developed over years, as each Unionist learned of another sympathizer to create links that accomplished these escapes.

William H. Brisby, a free African-American farmer, owned fifty acres in New Kent County and assisted many in leaving Richmond. He was a skilled blacksmith who had a pass that allowed him to enter and leave the city regularly. He drove a cart for his risky enterprise. Fugitives would lie down in the cart, and he covered them with something that was not recorded. But one night, he was arrested and taken to Castle Thunder. When nothing could be revealed to show his disloyalty, he was released. When he successfully spirited someone out of the city, he would take them to Yorktown and by boat to Union lines.

Samuel Ruth, a superintendent of the Richmond, Fredericksburg and Potomac Railroad, was the most unlikely Unionist of all. He was in charge

Cumberland Landing, 1862. Group of contrabands at Foller's house. *Library of Congress.*

Major General Benjamin F. Butler, USA. *Library of Congress.*

of the vital supply line for the Army of Northern Virginia. But he actually worked against the railway and the Confederate cause by slowing down trains and repairs to bridges. Robert E. Lee came forward as the primary accuser of Ruth's malfeasance. But Ruth demonstrated his cleverness by documenting periods of outstanding railway performance. Additionally, the railroad's owner, Peter V. Daniel Jr., remained convinced of Ruth's devotion to the CSA. His arrest was reported by the Richmond *Whig* on January 26, 1865:

> [A]*uthorities requested that for the present nothing should be said about the matter by the press. This request, we regret to say, has been disregarded by some of the city papers. Information obtained by the detective police led to the belief that Mr. Ruth had for a long time taken advantage of his position as Superintendent of the Richmond & Fredericksburg Railroad to convey important information to the enemy; and on Monday evening he was arrested on this charge and committed to Castle Thunder.*

There are too many stories related to spying, executions and escapes to retell them all here. The Richmond underground provided useful information to Union troops. General Butler became the primary contact with Richmond Unionists.

THE GREAT ESCAPE FROM LIBBY PRISON

What became known as the Great Escape could not have happened or been as successful as it was without Elizabeth Van Lew and her network of Unionists. In early 1864, two Union officers determined to escape Libby. They made a plan and did some work but failed after thirty-nine days to find a way out. Robert Ford, though a prisoner, was the hostler or stableman of the second in command of the prison, Dick Turner. Once the Union officers figured out an escape route, Rose provided key information on safe houses and even measured with twine how far they needed to tunnel to be safely out. We must skip the details, but suffice it to say that Elizabeth Van Lew and Abigail Green, another society lady, who assisted Van Lew, served as advisors and lined up others to help them escape to Union lines. On the night of February 9, 1864, and into the next day, 109 Union prisoners escaped through the tunnel. Other prisoners covered up the escape route and put things back in order in the cellar where the tunnel began.

After roll call the next morning, the escape was discovered. But it was more than twelve hours before troops were alerted of the escape and sent out to recapture prisoners. The escapees fanned out through the city to safe houses and were assisted in the coming days by both the underground network of Union loyalists in Richmond and by many African Americans in the region, slave and free, who guided them once they were outside the city. Fifty-nine of the escapees reached Union lines, forty-eight were recaptured and two drowned in their escape attempt. Sadly, Commander Turner suspected Robert Ford's complicity and had him whipped with five hundred lashes! Ford was laid up for six weeks after the severe torture. He managed to escape Libby in July 1864 and reach Washington, D.C., but no details of his escape are known. He was paid $814 by the government—pay he would have received in the army. Later, he was hired at the Department of Treasury, but he died in April 1869, partly due to complications from his beating.

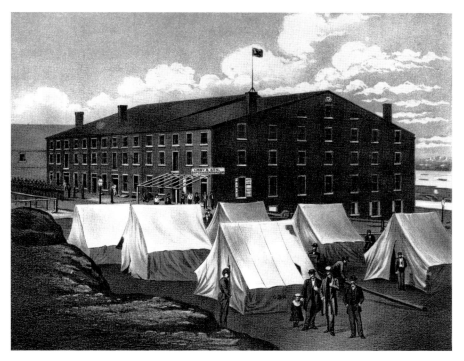

Libby Prison, as it appeared on August 23, 1863. *Library of Congress.*

Many freed African Americans assisted the Unionist efforts. Had they been found out, there would likely have been no arrests or trials but instead summary executions. The intelligence they gathered and passed on was invaluable. It was only through postwar newspaper investigations that detailed how the Richmond underground worked that we know many of these things. Many operatives were African Americans who carried passes that allowed them to bring goods and food into the city. They conveyed information via documents sewn into their coats and shoes with extra soles to allow for a hidden compartment and even stored messages inside hollowed-out eggshells.

While there were many Unionist activities showing character and courage, those who supported the Confederacy also stepped up to serve their cause. Who knows how many acts of kindness and sacrifice occurred in Confederate hospitals for next-door neighbors and to those who lost limbs in the war? A huge tragedy with many layers created stories that shall never be known.

Chapter 12

IMPORTANCE OF RICHMOND NEWSPAPERS

Newspapers were the Internet of antebellum America. Between 1830 and 1860, the number of newspapers in the United States (counting weeklies, circulars, dailies and more) exploded. The 1840 census counted 1,631 and the 1850 census 2,526; by the start of the Civil War, there were even more. There were already 254 daily newspapers in 1850, according to the American Antiquarian Society. Richmond was a prime example of an urban hub that witnessed this explosion of the printed word in dailies, weeklies, serials and subscription services.

The Civil War was a war of the printed word. Dating back to the pre-Revolutionary period in the American colonies, newspapers and related publications (serials, weeklies, broadsides and so on) were the primary (and sometimes only) means of communication across great distances. Newspapers could travel as fast as a man on horse, a coach or a packet boat could travel carrying the news. They served not just local or regional readerships but also often had a far greater reach up and down the East Coast. They were a fundamental element of democracy and self-governance. A letter could travel no faster than a newspaper:

> There were different types of papers for different audiences. Political papers were especially popular in this period. A political paper, as the name suggests, covered politics and government. For example, the Washington Globe was a political paper affiliated with Andrew Jackson's administration.[16]

New York newspaper correspondents' row. *Library of Congress.*

When the Continental Congress first met back in 1774, many individuals were amazed to meet face to face for the first time with the actual physical human beings whose words they had read for years or even decades. In a similar fashion, the newspapers and publications in the South wielded tremendous rhetorical leverage in comparison to the effect of local events and conversations. When the Confederate States government was formed, it was in part able to function and began to flourish due to the broad narrative power of the Southern press. The heart of that mostly free press would soon be centered in Richmond. Later, when the war effort faltered, the press would be a subject of sore controversy to those in positions of military or political authority.

By the Civil War, transmission and delivery times had been dramatically slashed by the invention of the railroad, telegraph and steam propulsion. Print technology itself had expanded to include more elaborate graphical representations and more types of text, as well as different types and sizes of paper, but standard broadsheet newspapers remained the normal daily means of news delivery. During the war, newspapers as a trade and information commodity were usually second in priority only to tobacco (Union) and coffee (Confederate) when soldiers lined up to trade across the lines or raided enemy camps.

Richmond immediately before and during the war was a city of newspapers, publishers and publications. The tradition of political activism and civic duty to knowledge stemmed from the colonial and Revolutionary experiences, where newspapers were the avenue of communication between distant cities down to networks of power within cities and readership circles.

TABLE 6. NEWSPAPERS AND SERIAL PUBLICATIONS IN WARTIME RICHMOND

Richmond Sentinel, office northeast corner of Governor and Franklin Streets, upstairs

Richmond Examiner, office west side of Governor Street, south of Franklin

Richmond Enquirer, office southwest corner of Main and Twelfth Street upstairs

Richmond Dispatch, office in Dispatch Building, corner of Main and Thirteenth Streets

Southern Illustrated News, office corner of Cary and Virginia Streets

The Magnolia, office opposite *Enquirer* office

Southern Punch, office on east side of Eleventh Street, south of Main

Southern Literary Messenger, office corner of Bank and Twelfth Streets

The Record, office at West & Johnston's book store, Main Street, between Twelfth and Thirteenth Streets

Religious Herald, office on west side of 10th Street, south of Main

Central Presbyterian, office No. 148, Main Street, upstairs

Richmond Christian Advocate, office over Bidgood's book store, opposite telegraph office

Southern Churchman, office over Woodhouse's book store, south side Main Street, near Thirteenth Street

Christian Observer, office in law building, Franklin street, near Twelfth Street

Source: 1863 Richmond Business Directory

The major newspapers in wartime Richmond were the *Dispatch*, the *Enquirer*, the *Examiner*, the *Sentinel* and the *Whig*. There were many other smaller publications that came and went, so the exact number of serial publications is difficult to identify. According to the Encyclopedia Virginia by the Virginia Humanities, "Confederate newspapers in Virginia during the American Civil War (1861–1865) served as vital, if often flawed, sources of reporting on the conflict, as organs of national propaganda, and as venues in which to attack or defend the administration of Confederate president Jefferson Davis."

An emphasis on literacy that was a much larger force in America before, during and after the war was also evident in Richmond. There was even a sanctioned regime reading room: the "Confederate Reading Room, south side 11th street, north of Main street" was listed in the 1863 business directory.

There were even specialized journals on technical themes like medical research:

> *This medical journal began being published in January 1864, and was a continuation of a pre-war publication, also edited by J.B. McCaw. McCaw solicited articles from surgeons across the Confederacy. This section contains articles about the journal as well as selected articles from it.*[17]

JOHN MONCURE DANIEL

John Moncure Daniel, executive editor of the Richmond *Examiner*, was born in Stafford, Virginia, in 1825. He had a talent from an early age for writing and would eventually demonstrate a singular giftedness in journalism as well. Although he was penniless and without prospects at one point due to family circumstance, by the age of twenty-two he was working for the Richmond *Examiner*, a popular weekly. A short time later, after rising to editor, he was a patron and publisher of works by Edgar Allan Poe.

Talented, opinionated and political, Daniel was appointed as a diplomat to the Kingdom of Sardinia in 1853 and was a firsthand witness to the events of the Second Italian War of Independence. His experience overseas informed his revolutionary perspectives, and when he returned to Virginia in early 1861, he was already predisposed to see the fledgling Confederate government as equally inspiring and revolutionary. He resumed control at the now daily newspaper in Richmond and was a strong supporter (initially) of newly elected president Jefferson Davis and the fledgling Confederate regime.

Daniel was also an early proponent of moving the Confederate capital to Richmond, but his relationship with the capital city ultimately proved fractious. He became the regime's greatest critic, lambasting everything from choice of generalships to nepotism in the awarding of government contracts. Between his editorial duties, Daniel also served twice in the military, being wounded the second time in the arm at Gaines's Mill in the Seven Days Battles.

Daniel's weakness was his vanity, and he was involved in several duels throughout his adult life. In 1864, after the *Examiner* reported on an alleged impropriety in the Confederate Treasury Department, Confederate treasurer Edward C. Elmore challenged Daniel to a duel, and in the ensuing confrontation Daniel received a serious leg wound. Ultimately, in March 1865, he succumbed to complications from the wounds and the treatment. He is buried at Hollywood Cemetery.

As the war wore on, resources from paper to type set (made from lead) became scarcer, and the ability of smaller locales to keep producing serial publications was greatly diminished. Even larger cities could not support the print infrastructure of prewar levels:

> When the war broke out in 1861, some 120 newspapers were published in Virginia. Every town of any size boasted at least a weekly paper. Richmond, a city of nearly 39,000 people, had four daily newspapers. Two years into the war, though, only seventeen of the state's papers were still in publication (and the attrition was not over). By mid-1864, outside Richmond and Petersburg, the number of pro-Confederate presses in the state could be counted on one hand.[18]

Confederate president Jefferson Davis could just not seem to avoid being in almost constant conflict with the media, sometimes even the pro-Confederate branch of it. One point of contention was the draft—publishers argued that their key staff should be exempt. At one point in the war, the *Southern Punch* was employing a deaf-mute, an amputee, a man with a lame arm and a Canadian—all in theory exempt. Yet the government always skimmed the system for more men, even those who could not perform front-line duty.[19]

Davis's conflict with the media went much deeper than the draft. On March 1, 1862, when Davis acted on a congressionally approved suspension of habeas corpus, the media felt conflicting loyalties. Historians such as Stephen Ash maintain that the free press was not unduly constrained, although anecdotal evidence suggests that many individuals, including those in the media, felt the actions went beyond simply finding Union sympathizers and securing safety from external threat.

Newspaper editors were some of the hottest heads in a hot city. Henry Pollard of the Richmond *Examiner* had to be temporarily saved from himself by the mayor:

> *Examination for Dueling.—Yesterday morning Messrs. Henry R. Pollard, of the* Examiner, *and Edward C. Elmore, late Confederate States Treasurer, arrested Tuesday evening on the charge of being about to engage in a duel with deadly weapons, were brought before the Mayor to answer the offence. Hon. Humphrey Marshall appeared as the counsel for Mr. Elmore, and Hon. Patrick Henry Aylett acted in the same capacity for Mr. Pollard. The Mayor, on calling the case, explained why it was that he had refused on the evening of the arrest to admit Mr. Elmore to bail. He stated that after Mr. Elmore had been taken into custody, he learned that he had shot Mr. Daniel in a duel on that day, which act constituted a felony, and therefore, he considered that the law in such cases necessitated committal. Mr. Pollard had been arrested and admitted to bail not on account of any offence he had committed; but for the purpose of preventing a hostile meeting which it was apprehended was about to take place between himself and Mr. Elmore. After this explanation, Messrs. George W. Butler, J. Marshall Hanna, and Dr. A.E. Petticolas were examined as witnesses for the Commonwealth.*[20]

After the Union occupation forces began to restore order in Richmond on April 3, after "evacuation day," some of the newspapers and local media almost immediately resumed production and reporting on the startling new circumstances. The Civil War, including the example set in Richmond, truly was the first media-driven war.

Chapter 13

STORIES AND INCIDENTS DURING
THE WAR YEARS

Richmond at war was a daily series of soap operas and individual vignettes that, considered together, defy a master narrative. Every day, for the most part, included at least one funeral, at least one marriage, an act of chivalry, an act of civil disobedience, an arrival of a wounded soldier, the passage of a new conscript, the sale of a slave, the breakdown of a train, the escape attempt of a POW or the passage of new legislation to sustain the war effort. It also included multiple crimes. It is through the vignettes that we can begin to piece together a pattern.

Richmond became a kind of frontier town more reminiscent of the Wild West than the conservative colonial tidewater. This was largely a result of the population explosion, the high number of temporary and transient residents and the lack of a law enforcement infrastructure to deal with what are arguably the normal good and bad foibles of a city population.

For much of the war, Provost Marshal Samuel Winder had responsibility—along with local authorities—for maintaining peace and calm in Richmond. A unique culture had grown up in the years of war, with excitement and energy gradually giving way to stubborn determination and quiet suffering. The glamorous balls became less frequent, while funerals became more frequent and food grew scarce. In spite of this, the city continued to function in all of its many roles. Everyday life in the Civil War was unique in countless ways.

JOHN LETCHER

John Letcher was born in Lexington, Virginia, in 1813 and studied at Randolph-Macon College in Boydton (the college moved to Ashland after the Civil War) and then at Washington Academy in Lexington, where he finished in 1833. He passed the bar and became an attorney, opening his practice in 1839. He soon went on to serve as editor of the *Valley Star* newspaper, a campaigner in a series of presidential elections and a member of the U.S. Congress; he developed a reputation for being honest and straightforward.

Letcher was elected governor of Virginia in 1859 and served to the end of his term in 1864. Although he is memorialized for his role in trying to stop the Bread Riot in 1863, he is in other ways a somewhat invisible figure during much of Richmond's high wartime drama—appearing for inspections and intervening on behalf of pardon requests but overshadowed by the dramatics of his successor, Extra Billy Smith, and other more flamboyant personalities.

He apparently was a good listener, as the records are filled with people making appeals to him for this kind of favor or that. After the war, his continued professional success confirmed this. He was elected to the Virginia General Assembly, resumed his law practice and served on the Board of Visitors for the Virginia Military Institute.

It is fair to say that he was a force for stability, whether it was something innocuous but critical like trying to facilitate the connection of rail lines between Richmond and Petersburg or something more annoying and forgotten like answering midnight calls at the door of the governor's mansion to react to some new war-related development.

BOY GANGS ("CATS")

With fathers and older teenage brothers almost all off to war service, mothers often employed directly or indirectly in the war effort and many schools shut down, it is no wonder that any male under the age of thirteen was more than likely to be bored, unless he could find his own piece of the action. Naturally, finding the action meant that boys often ended up in trouble or even court. Sometimes, local merchants used them for errands, message running and other small tasks at rates cheaper than hired-out labor, free or slave. But even that only covered so many hours of the day. Many diaries, letters and memories of the time mention their presence throughout the city.

MARRIAGE

As during almost any conflict, there were a number of prominent and rushed marriages during wartime in Richmond. According to Ward Carroll, "A flurry of marriages occurred early in the war, whenever men went on furlough, and then again at the end of the war. Richmond, the Confederate capital, hosted hundreds of wartime marriages, leading observers to marvel at the 'marriage frenzy.'"

Many soldiers held the prospect of marriage and settling down as a tonic daydream to counter the realities of muddy trenches, death and deprivation. Their plans were countered by the terrible reality of war: one in five Southern white males perished in the war, leaving many women fearful about marriage prospects. "Having made up my mind not to be an old maid," a woman called Hattie wrote, "and having only a modest fortune and less beauty. I fear I shall find it rather difficult to accomplish my wishes." The war only compounded her anxieties.[21]

Nevertheless, there were fleeting moments of happiness and celebration, accented by prominent partnerships that were the talk of the city. Even those moments, however, were subject to somber reminders of war. Mary Chesnut recalled an event at her friend Bettie Bierne's wartime wedding:

> We were among the first to arrive. Then came a faint flutter and Mrs. Parkman (the bride's sister, swathed in weeds for her young husband, who had been killed within a year of her marriage) came rapidly up the aisle alone. She dropped upon her knees in the front pew, and there remained, motionless, during the whole ceremony, a mass of black crepe, and a dead weight on my heart. She has had experience of war. A cannonade around Richmond interrupted her marriage service—a sinister omen—and in a year thereafter her bridegroom was stiff and stark—dead upon the field of battle.

Bettie's husband was Congressman William Porcher Miles, who also designed the version of the Confederate flag that became associated with the Army of Northern Virginia. Despite the shortage of men that women feared would limit their opportunities, men displaced by service or the whims of war also worried:

> WANTED—A WIFE—A soldier who has been wounded in defence of his country, and whose appearance, character, and habits, would not be disagreeable to any young lady, feeling lonely and in want of a companion,

makes an appeal to some member of the fair sex to come forward and fill the void in his heart. One capable of loving to an intense degree, accomplished and amiable, is preferred. Riches no object. Address "Q," box 234, Charlottesville, Va.[22]

Dueling

Like almost all antebellum Southern cities, Richmond had multiple dueling grounds. The most famous was located on Church Hill, along the east side of Thirtieth Street between Franklin and Grace. It was referred to as "Bloody Run" or "Chimborazo Heights." After the war, the Confederate section of the Oakwood cemetery was the site of duels. The last reported duel was in the 1890s.

Scores of deaths occurred over the decades, and dueling continued unabated during the war. A case in 1861 involving the death of Washington J. Worsham seemed to be reported fully: "The person who fired it was Jas. McCullough; time, Saturday morning; place, Broad Rock Race Course; occasion, a duel, at ten paces." But McCullough could not be located, and the jury ruled that Washington's killer was unknown.

Journalists seemed particularly susceptible to being baited into conflict (perhaps the nature of their investigative business). O. Jennings Wise, who was the editor of the Richmond *Enquirer* leading up to the war, fought eight duels as a result of his outspoken editorial aggression. He later died as a Union prisoner.

Mayor Mayo

Joseph Carrington Mayo was born in 1795 in Powhatan Seat, an area east of Richmond that is today within the Fulton neighborhood. Mayo's family was involved in many interesting aspects of Virginia's early history—his great-grandfather, for example, had helped survey the original city plots destined to become the city of Richmond. Joseph himself was fated to lead an interesting life, becoming a prominent attorney, civic booster, member of the Virginia House and eventually long-serving mayor of Richmond.

Mayo, who began serving as mayor in 1853, was part of many changes and improvements to the city, including new waterworks, new fire engines, completion of the new city gasworks (Fulton Gas Works, close to Rockett's Landing) and many public dedications, such as the 1858 unveiling of the famous Washington equestrian statue in Capitol Square. He also presided over the notorious "Mayor's Courts," which quickly gained a reputation for being "marked by cruelty and injustice" and were aimed mostly at controlling African Americans, both free and enslaved, as well as some poor whites.

Mayo continued as mayor during the war and was a figure in many prominent incidents and events, the most notable of which was the Bread Riot of early 1863. As a result of the riots, cannons were placed in key intersections and security was tightened. Mayo also oversaw some efforts at relief for the suffering population.

After the war, Mayo was in and out of office as mayor, depending on the whims of Union occupation officials and voters. His mental health soon declined, however, and he spent the end of his life in an insane asylum, passing away in 1872. He is buried at Shockoe Hill Cemetery.

RICHMOND BREAD RIOT OF 1863

The Richmond Bread Riot, also known as the Holy Thursday or the Women's Riot, turned out to be the largest civil disturbance in the Confederacy and occurred on April 2, 1863, exactly two years before the fall of Richmond. It proved to be a significant upheaval of the social order that foreshadowed an even greater cultural shift. The riots, led by Mary Jackson and joined by hundreds of other Richmond women, were, on the surface, about food shortages and runaway inflation. Deeper analysis, however, reveals an antebellum Southern culture splitting apart at the seams. The gender stereotypes of the time suggested that women should be submissive and quiet, relegated to mostly homemaker duties. Instead, the war helped to create a class of women who worked outside the home, began to manage family finances, often were widowed and who were capable of acting with strength and decisiveness.

Additionally, a massive snowstorm in March left roads impassable from mud. What little produce that was nearby could not make it to the city. The demands to support the Army of Northern Virginia always ratcheted upward in the spring. Jefferson Davis called for a day of Fasting and Prayer on March 27 that angered many poorer people. Here is an example of how people who had nothing to gain from supporting slavery felt the pain of the war.

Jackson planned the civil disobedience carefully in a manner that would be familiar to late nineteenth-century labor union organizers and twentieth-century identity rights leaders. One witness later referred to them as "female communists." Some were probably aware of other similar riots that were occurring throughout the South. There was a growing sense of solidarity before the riot even took place. She utilized networks, including large factories that employed women, to spread the word several weeks in advance.

The formal planning took place in Richmond with a meeting held on April 1 at the Belvidere Hill Baptist Church in Oregon Hill. It was decided at this meeting, made up primarily of working-class women, that they would demand food from the governor (some were willing to just get to pay the army price for goods instead of inflated consumer rates); if he didn't comply, they would simply take what they needed from merchants in the commercial district. They were told to arm themselves, which meant everything from rusty family pistols to hatchets and knives. It would happen the next day, April 2.

Mary Jackson, somewhat like a disgruntled action hero in a contemporary movie, showed up to work the next morning heavily armed and announced exactly what her intentions were. She also told several policemen. Apparently, none of these men tried forcefully to stop her, although they later reported they had advised her against the plan. Leaving Second Market, she picked up other protestors, many of them due to the previously organized plan, but the growing group also acquired spontaneous curiosity seekers or impulsive supporters. Richmond streets were always filled with those going somewhere, especially to market each day for food. A number of young boys, always looking for trouble due to their parents' new wartime roles, joined the crowd as it headed to Capitol Square.

Although there are different versions of events, there is general agreement that Governor Letcher did eventually address the crowd near the Washington statue when his aide, Bassett French, had been unable to satisfy the group. Letcher's appeal fell short, too, and the crowd proceeded to move down Ninth Street toward Main "in eerie silence." Some began to commandeer wagons in the street for the anticipated loot. At Cary Street, the looting began in earnest. "A toothless old woman" with an axe (Mary Johnson) broke into Pollard and Walker's and took five hundred pounds of bacon, and the riot moved into the looting phase.

The crowd proceeded from business to business, with the chaos that accompanies such unpredictable events. In one store, a woman reportedly broke the window and reached in only to have an angry merchant cut her fingers off. In another, a store owner waved women away with a loaded gun. Many of the women were seen wearing new shoes after the rioters passed a shoe store. Remarkably, no one was fatally injured. By this time, some men had also joined the group, which some sources cite as having grown to as large as one thousand or more people.

Mayor Joseph Mayo was the next to try to stop the chaos. He stood on an impromptu stand and literally read the riot act aloud, word for word, to no avail. President Jefferson Davis also addressed the crowd, without convincing them to stop. The mob continued down Cary, looting, and then back up to Main. In the meantime, the governor (or Davis, depending on the source) had called out the Public Guard, who were now marching down Main from the opposite direction, and when confronted with loaded guns and obvious military authority, the crowd began to disperse. The police played no decisive role in the affair. It was barely 11:00 a.m.

As soon as calm returned, the authorities were quick to go into action. Mary Jackson was arrested sometime around or just after noon. She would later be charged with a misdemeanor since it couldn't be proved that she stole anything herself personally. In all, incomplete records suggest that forty-one to forty-four women and twenty-four to twenty-nine men were arrested. Mary Jackson is lost in the records after November 1863. Many others paid fines and served relatively short jail terms. Some appealed for pardons or had charges dropped.

Confederate authorities tried in vain to keep the news from reaching the armies or the enemy. A short time after the riot, it was front-page news in some Northern newspapers. In many ways, the genie could not be put back in the bottle. The desperation of the times was unable to be addressed, however, simply because it was physically impossible to meet basic needs. William Blair, in *Virginia's Private War*, recounting the situation a few months later after Gettysburg, showed that the situation for many women had not changed, as office clerks who were drafted had to be replaced:

> In Richmond, officials visited homes to interview people requesting employment with the quartermaster's bureau. A list of ten women under consideration included wives of men in a variety of occupations: a carpenter, a stonemason, a member of the city watch, a soldier, and a worker in a government laboratory. The rest lived with children or other dependents without visible means of support. They constituted only a portion of the hundreds of destitute women who petitioned the government for work, often to no avail.

SEX IN RICHMOND IN THE CIVIL WAR

A taboo topic in mainstream antebellum norms, sex became something that was of great concern in terms of both civil governance and military organization, ranging from the rapid proliferation of prostitution in Richmond to the equally rapid spread of venereal diseases among soldiers ("One night with Venus; A lifetime with Mercury"). Also, a crisis of marriage increasingly written about today by contemporary sociologists resulted from almost all eligible males departing for military service, followed by one in three of the prime age range dying before they could raise a family. Even at the time, newspapers and private diaries began to fill with communicated fears that there would not be enough eligible husbands and therefore no way to provide for or have families.

Prostitution became an insoluble problem in Richmond. Wherever large numbers of soldiers concentrated, prostitution appeared simultaneously. Whenever Mayor Joseph Mayo found out about an obvious concentration of prostitution, he was compelled to act, as in this 1861 report:

> *Complained Of.—A row of houses in rear of the Exchange Hotel, occupied by parties of a dubious and uncertain character, is the prolific source of many a disgraceful row which the police have been called on to quell. The testimony given in a case before the Mayor Tuesday, proved the houses alluded to contain many nests of vile and unclean birds. The Mayor intimated his intention of having the houses cleaned of their present occupants.*[23]

But efforts were mostly in vain, as supply and demand were ever present. Drastic tactics included unannounced raids by the assistant provost marshal and his men. The problem got worse as the war dragged on, exacerbated by the scarcity of food and inflation of the Confederate currency. The system rewarded those working in black markets. The numbers became so great that a special department was created to hold prostitutes at Castle Thunder.

Once when two female prostitutes were making lewd gestures for the benefit of soldiers on duty at Libby Prison (and presumably some of the prisoners there too), and before matters got out of hand, the commanding officer incarcerated the women in the prison for the night, where they could "commune with their own thoughts." The YMCA found that women of the night had taken up residence next to its philanthropic efforts and complained that "the attention of their patients is very much diverted from their legitimate business." Presumably the provost's office investigated the "half-nude" women advertising for recovering soldiers. Several well-known prostitutes were arrested while in a private booth at the Marshall Theatre (they were discovered thanks to a respectable male recognizing them). Women wishing to keep their identity secret at night often dressed as men.

Gender roles began to blur during the war as the entire population shifted to a war footing. Women dressed more like men as they adapted to labor in the factory. There are many cases of crossdressing reported during the war, and not just as spies or POWs trying to escape:

> *Extraordinary Freak—Considerable excitement was occasioned on 12th street, below Main, yesterday afternoon, by the appearance of a man dressed in women's clothing. He soon made himself scarce, and the police did not succeed in tracing him to his hiding place.*[24]

In a turnabout case, a woman from Washington, D.C., named Maria Underwood was sent to Castle Thunder when she attempted to dress and pass as a man and then enlist in the Palmetto Sharpshooters. The second physical exam caught her ruse, although the paper suspected that "the conduct of the would-be son of Mars is not attributable to a love of adventure, but is regarded as the effect of the tender passion [for a soldier in the regiment]."[25]

There were many such incidents:

> *Tennella Green, a boarder at Ann Thomas's, on Cary street, was arraigned for appearing at the Varieties in men's clothes. She was let off, it appearing to be nothing more than the practical execution of a whim on her part.*[26]

Late in the war, two women from southwestern Virginia were brought to Castle Thunder for impersonating male soldiers—they had fought in Jubal Early's army for two years! Sometimes appearances were doubly deceiving. A man was once mistaken for a woman dressed as a man:

> *Supposed Female Proved to be a Man.—A very feminine-looking party stopped at the American Hotel a few days since, whose appearance led to the suspicion that it was a lady dressed in male apparel. A detective of the Eastern District was engaged to arrest the woman—if it was a woman,—but as it proved to be a real man, no arrest was made; and the scandal of having a fast young lady in male attire in the house was proved to be groundless.*[27]

Sexually aberrant behavior came in many forms. John Taylor was sent to jail in 1862 for exposing himself in public, as was Emanuel Olliberg for the same thing. In the same year, a woman was arrested for "indulging in horseback exercise"—a euphemism that actually sounded harmless until one realizes later in the account that she was overtly mimicking sex acts. Another man likely caught masturbating was said in court to have "got drunk in his room and made manifestations contrary to law and good manners." It was not uncommon to find white men arrested for visiting mixed-race or African-American prostitutes, in which case both parties were charged— the men with the crime of "associating with negros" and the women with prostitution. White women who "associated" with African-American men were subject to jail time, while their companions often received "35 lashes." Of course, what got reported in papers likely amounted to a fraction of a fraction of what went on. In a town where you have no family and few know you, we would expect such a breakdown of prior norms. Plus, soldiers were on leave and wives or girlfriends were hundreds of miles away.

At Ruskell's Stable, fourteen women were arrested for prostitution in one night (including one woman sixty years old). "The women, during the day, exposed their persons in the windows, and halloed at, threw at and spit upon all passersby. But when the sun went down arrived the time for the exercise of their most disagreeable practices. They got drunk and made night hideous with their maudlin revelry." The police, upon arrival, found "the woman and men behaving themselves in a manner calculated to disturb the peace and quiet of the neighborhood."

Slaves rented out to factories in Richmond, enjoying a relatively broader degree of freedom, often found trouble at houses of ill repute run by other free African Americans, as did slaves working in the city to earn extra income. All were subject to prosecution.

Homosexuality was another taboo subject, but nevertheless, it crops up occasionally in the records. An angry citizen editorializing about the moral decay of the city in 1862 decried "the imprudence and familiar vulgarity of many of the shamefaced of the prostitutes of both sexes" who roamed the streets freely. On the Union side, one soldier wrote home about sleeping with one of the drummers in his unit. But generally, records on both sides don't indicate any formal punishment for same-sex love, and the terminology for describing it was different and forbidden (unless you were Walt Whitman), so the subject remains largely unrecorded in Richmond or anywhere else. Some of these instances likely mirrored the behavior of straight males who are incarcerated and use men as surrogates for women.

The crime of rape—unacceptable under any circumstance—was frequently reported in newspapers. It often resulted in serious punishments, including and up to death. There is no way to know for sure—since official documents only record a fraction of the sexual assaults that actually occurred—but it does seem clear that the overcrowded, stressful and dangerous conditions of wartime Richmond increased the number significantly. Men charged with rape were also brought to Richmond from other areas to be punished or processed, such as "Henry Rapur, a Yankee, charged with rape" in late 1862, who was transferred from Staunton, Virginia, to Castle Thunder.

A sampling from lists of known areas of ill repute includes such interesting names as "house of ill-fame" in Butchertown, "sinful abode" of Ella Johnson (rear of Exchange), the Ann E. Thomas Bawdy House or "House of Evil Fame," "Solitude" (an area on Cary Street), the Bell Jones House, Highland Row Rockett's and so on. Locations changed constantly, but at any given time there were probably several dozen brothels in operation, or more.

DEATH AND DYING IN CIVIL WAR RICHMOND

The Richmond *Whig* on May 2, 1864, reported the death of Joseph Davis, son of Varina and President Jefferson Davis, on April 30. The four-year-old boy stepped over a railing on a porch at the White House of the Confederacy and fell about twelve feet onto a granite border below the porch. Similarly, Mary Todd and President Lincoln lost their son Willie to typhoid fever in February 1862. Both presidents lost a young child during the war.

On January 19, 1865, General John Pegram married Hetty Cary at St. Paul's Episcopal Church in a joyous wedding ceremony. Jefferson Davis loaned his carriage to take the couple to their honeymoon at a farmhouse near the groom's command at Petersburg. A few weeks later, on February 6, John Pegram lay dead in the snow. Exactly three weeks after his marriage, his coffin occupied the same place he stood to be married. Mrs. John Pegram stood there, this time covered in black crepe.

Throughout the war, widows and mothers had been making trips to Richmond to reclaim the remains of husbands, fathers, brothers and other male relations such as close relatives or fiancés. Casket making must have been an in-demand business.

As wartime Richmond grew in population to well over 100,000 inhabitants, the destruction of the Civil War naturally brought record levels

St. Paul's Episcopal Church (known
as the Cathedral of the Confederacy).
Photo by Derek Kannemeyer.

of death to Richmond. Not only did people in Richmond pass away due to old age and sometimes due to hardship and epidemic, but also many dead soldiers returning home southward passed through on their way for burial—many soldiers were buried directly at the cemeteries here. Battles near the city created crisis periods when deaths were literally counted in the form of hundreds or even thousands of corpses that quickly had to be dealt with. Mass graves or unmarked graves had to be employed.

Historians argue periodically over the actual mortality of the war, military and civilian. Current estimates are clustered around the number 750,000 (according to J. David Hacker, a demographic historian from Binghamton University in New York, in 2012), with about 50,000 being war-related civilian casualties and the rest being military deaths (including combat, accident and the largest killer of all, disease). During a normal prewar year, the raw mortality rate could average between 20 to 40 per 1,000, although this is still a crude estimate; this would mean that in 1860, roughly 500,000 or more Americans would be dying in the natural course of things from old age, accidents, childbirth, illness and so on. If you combine the war and natural mortality during 1861–65, it can quickly be seen that death would affect almost every family in the country, especially in Richmond.[28]

Over the course of the war, more than eighteen thousand Confederate soldiers were buried at Hollywood Cemetery alone. Burials at Hollywood Cemetery were frequent enough that twelve full-time grave diggers were employed, and the superintendent complained vehemently when there was an attempt to draft some of them into the army. The cemetery had to be expanded during the war. Among the most famous Confederates interred at Hollywood are President Jefferson Davis (1889), General J.E.B. Stuart (1864) and General George Pickett (1875). In addition, two U.S. presidents (Monroe and Tyler) and six Virginia governors are among the countless politicians interred there. Jefferson Davis died in 1889 and was buried in New Orleans. Varina Davis, his widow, thought that he should be buried in Hollywood Cemetery with so many other Confederates there. He was reinterred in Richmond on May 31, 1893. Veterans set bonfires beside the tracks that brought President Davis's body to Richmond and escorted the caisson to Hollywood Cemetery. Mrs. Davis also buried their children who died before her, except Isaac Cook Davis, who died at the Battle of Stones Creek. The couple had six children. Her last child, Margaret Howell Davis Hayes, died after her but requested to be buried with her mother and father.

Many visitors to wartime Richmond noted how the women seemed to perpetually dress in black and nothing else. Letters and diary entries often record women making requests from other parts of the South for black material to be sent to them to make more mourning garb. A number of famous wartime photographs in Richmond show women covered in black solemnly traversing the streets. In 1865, a New York correspondent wrote, "It was mournful to walk about the city. So many houses deserted, so many ladies in mourning—all I met were in mourning—so many old men, broken with premature age, their hats made respectable by the dingy crape that told of sons slain, and then that broad black waste where stood the busiest part of the city—it was pitiful."[29]

The average American life expectancy in 1860 was from around thirty-nine to forty-five, depending on how infant mortality is factored in, so Americans already were relatively accustomed to death. The average Union soldier was just under twenty-six. While the average Confederate soldier's age is not known, it was probably younger than twenty-six in the first half of the war and older in the second half. It is suggested that as many as several hundreds of thousands of men (really boys) under the age of twenty served on both sides during the course of the war. With one in four soldiers on each side perishing (as many as one in three in the South), and with estimates of more than five hundred deaths per day on average, it is safe to say that the city

Hebrew Cemetery, Confederate dead (Shockoe Hill). *Photo by Misti Nolen.*

of Richmond as the focus of the Union invasion effort, and the penultimate Confederate organizational hub, could have averaged as many as fifty deaths per day that either occurred in hospitals or were directly a result of nearby battlefield casualties; occurred in POW camps (one hundred were buried at Shockoe Hill Cemetery alone in a short number of days in 1861); were part of civilian attrition; or were bodies passing through on their way to home burial in other parts of the South. Richmond, by all accounts, was a city consumed by death. At peak times after major battles, that number would have been in the many hundreds or more per day.

At Oakwood Cemetery, 540 Confederate soldiers were buried in the first six months of the war (roughly 16,000 eventually). More than 1,000 people (civilian, soldier, POW and so on) were buried in Shockoe Hill Cemetery the first part of the war, with one newspaper saying it was "explained in part, by the mortality among volunteers and other strangers. It must also be remembered that the population of the city is rapidly increasing." Shockoe Hill Cemetery commonly averaged more than 500 male burials per quarter.

Death by accident occurred all the time in wartime Richmond as well:

> *"Drunken butcher falls into the canal and drowns"* [there were numerous canal drownings during the war]; *"[D]eath at Tredegar—man falls down a flight of steps"; "[S]oldiers encamped near Hollywood Cemetery are requested not to fire their weapons into the cemetery, after funeral*

attendee is struck by a spent bullet"; "2 guards [civilians] at Louisiana Hospital fight—one kills the other [accidentally]"; "A youth about 14 years of age, named George Mathews, son of Mr. Mathews, of Jackson street, was killed yesterday, about 5 o'clock, by being run over by the wood train"; "Two workmen were fatally injured in a shed at the Tredegar Iron Works on Saturday, by the falling of the roof which was mashed by an accumulated mass of snow"; "Andrew Marsden, a discharged Arkansas volunteer, recently received as a patient at the Richmond Medical Hospital, arose from his bed, at that institution, Tuesday night, and in passing through a dark passage, walked into a sort of hatchway, fell to the floor below, and was instantly killed."[30]

Drowning in the canal basin, or river, was such a risk that eventually authorities were forced by circumstances to take some kind of action. One of their reported improvements: "Space on either side of the canal bridge on 8th street to be fenced in, in order to prevent accidents." A drunken mother fell into the canal in 1862 and lost her baby to drowning, although she survived in spite of her inebriated state. It was not uncommon to recover decomposed bodies that had drowned months earlier, white or African American. Sometimes they were identifiable by uniform.

Suicide, while a relatively taboo subject in antebellum America, also occurred with alarmingly frequency during the war (and as a result entered into a larger medical and psychological dialogue):

Suicide.—Lieut. C.E. Earle, of the Palmetto Guard, of Col. Sloan's 4th Regiment of South Carolina volunteers, killed himself instantly yesterday evening, about 4 o'clock, by jumping from the eastern 6th story window of the Ballard House, fronting on Franklin street. Lieut. Earle fell a distance of about one hundred and ten feet to the pavement below, breaking his skull in several places, also his arm and legs.

Geo. Sheridan, Ala. soldier, goes crazy, runs through streets in underwear, leaps to death in canal at "Armory Bridge."

Suicide of a Soldier.—A soldier who had been for some weeks confined by indisposition to his bed at Chimborazo Hospital, cut his throat on Monday night. The reporter is informed that the deceased asked for a furlough to go home, and not obtaining it, resorted to the desperate expedient of taking his own life.[31]

There are almost as many accounts of attempted suicide that failed for one reason or another. In October 1863, Henri Garidel, who worked for the War Department, began to have thoughts about taking his own life. Only his strong Catholic faith and desperate love for his family back in New Orleans kept him going.[32]

Some relatively uncommon causes of death were recorded as well:

> *We regret to learn that Mr. Philip Rahm, proprietor of the "Eagle Foundry," in this city, died yesterday morning, at his residence, on 8th street, from lockjaw.*

> *Accidentally Killed.—S.W. Glover, of Buckingham county, Va., a member of company K, 41st Virginia regiment, was killed on Monday night last, while a passenger for this city on one of Edmond & Co.'s canal packets. While standing on the deck of the boat his head came in contact with a sleeper in Mr. Samuel Cottrell's bridge, by which his neck was broken.[33]*

There were many cases of industrial accidents, including the tragic 1863 explosion at the Confederate Ordnance Laboratory already described elsewhere in the book. The newspapers were literally filled with obituaries immediately after that tragedy. It was far from the only case, however:

> *Explosion of Fulminating Powder—Man Killed. A large mass of fulminating powder exploded about 11 o'clock yesterday, in the wooden house used for its manufacture, on Brown's Island, in James river, at the foot of 7th street, and instantly killed and dreadfully mangled William Pratt, of Washington D.C., the party engaged in its manufacture.[34]*

Some "cold cases" never got resolved:

> *The body of a soldier, supposed from his dress to be from Louisiana, rose to the surface of the Dock yesterday, near the corner of 20th street, and though much decomposed, was secured to the bank, in order that the Coroner might hold an inquest over the remains.[35]*

Death by violence increased greatly during the war. Assault and murder rates steadily rose. Not even children were immune: "Coroner Sanxay yesterday held an inquest on 8th street, over the body of Patrick Carney, the lad who was so badly wounded on Saturday evening, by a ball shot across the basin at a lot of wild ducks sailing on its surface, by some person unknown."[36]

The violence also included a growing number of legally ordered executions for civilian and military crimes:

> *Three men are to expiate their offences to-day in or near this city by sudden and ignominious deaths. Michael Bucton, condemned at the last term of Judge Lyons's Court for the murder of John Delaney in December last, will suffer at the usual place of execution, below the Powder Magazine, between the hours of ten and two o'clock....James Broderick and Michael Kearns, members of the Letcher artillery, will suffer death by musketry, between the hours of 2 and 3 o'clock, at Camp Lee in presence of all their brother soldiers in the vicinity of the city, they having been condemned to death for the crime of desertion by the Court-Martial now in session here.* [37]

Another category included high-profile homicides:

> *A fatal shooting affray occurred in this city yesterday, about two o'clock, resulting in the almost instant death of R.E. Dixon, of Georgia, Clerk of the Confederate House of Representatives, by the hands of R.S. Ford, of Kentucky, Journal Clerk of the House.* [38]

Death became so routine that there was even a brief scare that the still-yet-living were actually being taken for burial before they were really deceased. The Richmond *Dispatch* debunked this, reporting that the "instances the bodies of persons (soldiers) not dead had been sent to one of the cemeteries for burial" were actually false and now disproven. There were even editorials debating about what to do with the many personal belongings of the deceased who could not be identified or soldiers with no close relatives. In 1862, the Richmond *Enquirer* expressed outrage at the number of unburied bodies lying around at Oakwood Cemetery awaiting interment. Another account claimed that soldiers there were being buried three men deep per grave due to lack of space and laborers.

The neglect sometimes became almost criminal:

> *Neglect of the dead is sometimes unavoidable in these times, but we can see no reason under any possible conjunction of circumstances to allow the body of one of our soldiers to lay for two days on the platform of the York River Railroad Depot without the slightest effort being made for its interment. A blanket and an open platform is not exactly the sort of treatment he should receive. The body of the soldier above alluded to was on the platform Wednesday evening, and had been there for two previous days.* [39]

Evidence exists even of infanticide—for example, the body of a small infant was found floating in the mill trace between Haxell's Mill and the Danville Depot. A coroner's officer investigated, but it's not clear that anything definitive or a suspect was ever found out.

Like all people in human history under the duress of war, Richmonders found various ways to cope with death, ranging from denial to alcoholism. Many retreated into religious comforts and even forms of more abstract spiritualism that presaged a larger postwar movement. Ghostly sightings of loved ones who were recently deceased are reported quite often in diaries and letters. People usually had to carry on without experiencing the normal period of time to mourn. Sufficient mourning was often impossible because other deaths of friends or loved ones occurred so soon after. As a result, many people began to become increasingly numb to the seemingly endless march of human destruction. The government awarded contracts to companies to bury (or dispose of) wartime victims of smallpox. Undertakers tried new body preservation techniques while waiting for loved ones from out of town to arrive for a deceased soul. And through all of this, government and military record keepers struggled to keep up with recording it all. Death was the business of the day.

A GOOD DEATH

Southerners (and Americans in general) had a somewhat different concept of a "good death" in the 1860s compared to Americans today. In general terms, a good death occurred at home (not a hospital), surrounded by loved ones (not medical personnel), without pain (the South had a chronic and devastating shortage of medicines and drugs) and with some sense of time to say goodbye to everyone and the world. It also included preparation for burial and a commemoration or funeral. Many wartime deaths in Richmond were missing most or even all of these hoped-for elements. This lack of ability to experience "good death" only increased collective mental stress and fatigue.

The capitalist "business" of death flourished. According to Stephen Ash and many others, the number of undertakers in or doing business with Richmond multiplied several times. Families in other parts of the South often spent sizable amounts of money having their loved ones shipped home for interment. One company, Bower's Foundry, located at Ninth and Cary, even began manufacturing a sealed metal coffin that would better preserve bodies on long journeys home (and would better contain smells, according to Stephen Ash).

Funerals became a macabre form of social interaction verging on entertainment. When someone famous passed away—such as General Stonewall Jackson—the body might lie in state and be accompanied by funeral marches and elaborate services. In Jackson's case, his departure for a final funeral service and burial in Lexington, Virginia, was also preceded by an elaborate ceremony and procession in Richmond, with a "wailing dirge" that accompanied his remains to the train station. One editorial lamented that the great hero would not be interred at Hollywood Cemetery with others of the Confederate cause. But most funerals, if they even occurred, were much simpler, shorter and without any pomp or circumstance. The vast number of people who died had no service at all.

Freed African Americans practiced within their Richmond community as many elements of the "good death" as they were capable of and legally permitted to do. But slaves, hundreds of whom perished in the war in or around Richmond, were almost never memorialized formally or given any of funereal formalities. It would require many generations for Richmonders of all backgrounds to begin to heal from the trauma of endless death during those years. The tens of thousands buried in Richmond—African American or white, male or female, old or young—remain unidentified in those same cemeteries today as a solemn reminder of those times.

PART III

Richmond in Decline, 1864–1865

Chapter 14

THE UNION WAR OF ATTRITION

The framework of the war changed in the spring of 1864 when Grant was promoted to general-in-chief with a rank of lieutenant general (a title only George Washington ever held) by Lincoln, who by creating this new position put Grant in charge of all Union forces everywhere. Grant did not believe and never studied Jomini's theories. He knew that to end the war, he had to destroy the Army of Northern Virginia. General George Gordon Meade, commander of the Army of the Potomac, was not the greatest general but pressed on with Grant's orders. Meade was the titular commander of the Army of the Potomac, but Grant gave the primary strategic orders.

Grant's overall strategy across the Confederacy was a "strategy of exhaustion" designed to strike at its logistical and industrial capacity. There was no desire or need to occupy territory. Union forces employed tactics of destroying crops, tearing up railroads, burning any manufacturing and rendering useless anything that might still aid the enemy. Once that was done, there was no need to leave troops in place to occupy those areas. It was different from a strategy of attrition, which seeks to reduce an enemy's manpower by inflicting casualties in battle. Grant's plan in Virginia was for Meade to tie down the Army of Northern Virginia wherever he could while waiting for an opportunity to completely destroy Lee's army. Also, General Butler, leading the Army of the James (newly formed from various Union corps in April 1864), would advance against Richmond from the south. But none of Grant's plans succeeded. Butler got within seven miles of Richmond but was rebuffed at Drewry's Bluff. But unlike McClellan, Butler remained in the area at Bermuda Hundred.

Clashes between Lee and Grant took place at the Wilderness May 5–6 and at Spotsylvania Court House between May 8 to May 21, 1864. At the Wilderness on May 5, Lee's army encountered Union forces that took the initiative and drove the rebels back to an intersection in the dense woods they would need to hold to attack Lee's flank. The next day, General Longstreet's division arrived to reinforce Lee. The Confederates knew of an overgrown railway bed they could use to get around the Union flank. Confederates surprised the enemy, but in the confusion, Longstreet got shot in the shoulder by friendly fire. He was not killed but instead was kept out of his post for five months. Both sides were exhausted from the fierce fighting. Under these circumstances, previous Union generals withdrew, but instead, Grant sent a telegram to Lincoln that said, "[W]hatever happens, there will be no turning back."

At Spotsylvania Court House, Lee's army built almost impregnable defenses. The Army of the Potomac sent wave after wave against the fortifications. At the end of days of fighting, the losses on both sides were horrific—thirty thousand casualties, with the most on the Union side. At this point, there becomes little need to report which side was the victor in each battle because the fighting continued and just moved to a new location. This level of losses suffered on the Union side caused prior generals to withdraw rather than lose more men. But Meade, following Grant's strategy, did not back off. On May 11, Grant sent a dispatch to Washington that read, "I am sending back to Belle Plain all my wagons for a fresh supply of provisions and ammunition and I propose to fight it out on this line, if it takes all summer." Grant was a different general than all who came before him. He used only one gear of his machine: forward. Lee did not have the same options for resupply that Grant did.

The narrative changes from all the engagements of previous years. Armies would fight campaigns and then withdraw, producing a period of calm. No longer would that be the way the Union army acted. Grant went after Lee. Grant continued south in pursuit of the Army of Northern Virginia. To Lee's credit, he continued his habit of entrenching his forces, as he had done when he took over the army. He was also better at accurately anticipating Grant's moves than Grant was at predicting Lee's. Lee built fortifications at Cold Harbor just outside Richmond near the old Gaines's Mill battleground. On June 3, Grant launched a massive attack that gained nothing but cost thousands. Grant received much criticism for this in the

Northern press, but because he had Lincoln's backing, he would not be replaced. Union casualties were 44,000 to 24,000 for the CSA. The likely population of Richmond was 100,000 in 1864, so those Confederates killed or wounded equaled almost a quarter of the city's population. This went on over and over for these four years.

Grant moved his army quickly over the James River and down to Petersburg, which had substantial physical fortifications but was not backed by large numbers of troops. General P.G.T. Beauregard, commander in Petersburg, sent messages to Lee asking for reinforcements. Fooled by Grant's move, Lee waited several days before rushing troops to Petersburg. But Union forces—plagued by exhaustion, poor leadership and reluctance to assault fortifications sturdier than Cold Harbor—caused a delay. By June 19, the opportunity for easy success had slipped by. Grant then settled into a long siege that would last the next nine months.

Events outside Richmond would now affect the city and the CSA more than ever before, driven by Grant's strategy of exhaustion. Briefly, the events taking place between August and October 1864, directed by Grant but carried out by General Philip H. Sheridan in the Shenandoah Valley and General William T. Sherman in Georgia, cemented the victory of the Union. There were several overlapping initiatives in the second half of 1864. While they didn't all take place near Richmond, the combination of events from Maryland to Georgia would cause the fall of Richmond.

General Philip Sheridan proved himself in the Western Theater over and over from 1861 through 1863, first as a staff officer and then as a brigadier general. His first major victory as a commander was the Battle of Booneville, Mississippi, July 1, 1862. Sheridan also performed brilliantly at the Battle of Chattanooga, supporting General George Thomas. This brought him to the notice of Chief of Staff Henry W. Halleck, who recommended him to Grant. Sheridan arrived to take charge of the Cavalry Corps of the Army of the Potomac on April 5, 1864. He followed orders, did not retreat and showed leadership on the field of battle.

Grant could not tolerate Confederate general Jubal Early's raids aimed at Washington. Early overcame small, uncoordinated attacks by Union forces from Lynchburg, up through the Valley of Virginia, outside Frederick, Maryland, and even threatened Washington. Lincoln went out to see the battle, and his stovepipe hat kept popping up as he stood to peer over the parapets. One captain, Oliver Wendell Holmes Jr., shouted, "Get down, you damn fool, before you get shot!" Lincoln did as he was told this time. Early's troops levied ransom in the towns of Hagerstown, where he received $20,000 in greenbacks and another $200,000 in Frederick. On July 30, 1864, two brigades of his cavalry demanded $500,000 from the citizens of Chambersburg, Pennsylvania. When they refused to pay what the Confederates called restitution for destruction in Virginia, they burned the town down.

On July 18, Lincoln issued a new call for 500,000 men, with quota deficiencies to be filled by a draft. This new draft and Jubal Early's attacks so close to Washington, along with the lack of success at Richmond and Atlanta, caused a lot of political heartburn for Lincoln, and Grant was not unaware of how politics affected his command. But frustrated by Washington red tape, Grant put Philip H. Sheridan in charge of the newly created Army of the Shenandoah. The triumvirate of Grant, Sheridan and Sherman would bring the war to its final conclusion. Sheridan had to consolidate and reorganize his forces for a few months in the critical summer of 1864.

THE BATTLE OF THE CRATER

The Army of the Potomac was not idle at Petersburg. The Forty-Eighth Pennsylvania regiment from coal country suggested to dig a tunnel under the Confederate lines and blow up the line. Work began in June but progressed slowly because materials were scarce. The regiment even built a ventilation shaft to bring in fresh air. The Confederates suspected that something was going on but did not give it full credence. However, Confederate general John Pegram, whose batteries he suspected would be above a possible explosion, took the threat seriously enough to build a new line of trenches and artillery points behind his position as a precaution. Finally, Grant and Meade approved the plan.

Burnside began to put much hope into the effort since his reputation had suffered much from his poor performance at Fredericksburg and at Spotsylvania Court House. The tunnel was 511 feet long, ending in a T-shape with two lateral tunnels 40 feet long under Confederate lines. The tunnel was loaded with eight thousand pounds of gunpowder. On July 30, they lit the fuse, but poor-quality materials required troops to go in and discover the place where the splice had failed. Finally, the explosion occurred at almost five o'clock in the morning. The explosion killed 278 Confederate soldiers and created the crater that can still be seen today on visits to the site. Poor execution and perhaps planning by Union leaders caused the attack to be delayed, and then their efforts were plagued by lack of leadership by James H. Ledlie, who was an alcoholic. The Confederates recovered from the shock to reorganize and start a counterattack. Union troops, rather than fanning out as planned, congregated in the middle of the Crater. With no leadership from Burnside, Union troops were like fish in a barrel. Both Burnside and Ledlie were relieved of their commands. The Union suffered another 4,000 casualties and had nothing to show for all of the effort. Meanwhile, Sherman fought John Bell Hood's forces around Atlanta.

The Battle of Atlanta Impacts Richmond

Atlanta sits only about one hundred miles from Chattanooga—about the same distance as Washington from Richmond. Grant and Sherman saw the opportunity. Atlanta had about ten thousand inhabitants in 1860, but its population had doubled to about twenty thousand by 1864 as manufacturing increased there as well. Atlanta, though not as large as Richmond, was a railroad hub and either manufactured or warehoused and shipped items used by the army. The Battle of Atlanta is too lengthy to be covered here. Fortifications around Atlanta rebuffed Sherman's effort to take the city. He changed plans and withdrew his army from its trenches going south of Atlanta to destroy the railroads. Union forces tore up tracks, heated the rails in large fires and wrapped the hot rails around trees, rendering them useless forever. These were called "Sherman neckties." He then marched north. Atlanta fell on September 2, 1864, and ensured Lincoln's reelection, which would ensure the continuation of Grant's command as well.

Sheridan and the Valley of Virginia

After the Battle of the Wilderness, Sheridan headed out to engage the Confederate cavalry under J.E.B. Stuart. From May 9 to May 24, 1864, Sheridan tried to threaten Richmond. Sallie Brock Putnam only mentioned Sheridan in her diary because at an encounter at Yellow Tavern, J.E.B. Stuart was shot and later died. He was only thirty-one years old. May 11 was a sad day for the Confederacy to lose not only such a capable general but also the verve and the sparkle that he possessed. Stuart was the last of the

Virginia cavaliers. But Sheridan never successfully threatened Richmond. The following month, he fought against Confederate major general Wade Hampton in the largest all-cavalry clash of the war between June 11 and June 12 in the Battle of Trevilian Station in Louisa County. Going west on Interstate 64 from Richmond, markers indicate the exit to see the area where the battle occurred. It was a Confederate victory in that Union forces did not succeed in destroying the Virginia Central Railroad or linking up with Union major general David Hunter in Charlottesville but instead retreated. But it may have been enough of a distraction to allow Grant to cross the James River after Cold Harbor.

After Sheridan assumed command of the Army of the Shenandoah in the summer of 1864, things changed for him. Sheridan's attacks against Jubal Early's forces put an end to that threat. The Union achieved a series of successes in the Valley. He won important victories at Third Winchester on September 19, Fisher's Hill on September 22 and the famous battle of Cedar Creek on October 19. After Fisher's Hill, Sheridan began to implement Grant's second directive. Grant's first directive was to follow Early "to the death." The second directive was to turn "the Shenandoah Valley [into] a barren waste…so that crows flying over it for the balance of this season will have to carry their provender with them." Like Sherman's March to the Sea, on September 26 Sheridan's forces began destroying crops and barns, rendering the "breadbasket of the Confederacy" empty just as the summer harvest had concluded. What was known as "the burning" began at Harrisonburg on September 26 and concluded thirteen days later on October 8 at Fisher's Hill. Sheridan reported by October 7 that they had "destroyed over 2,000 barns filled with wheat, hay, and farming implements; over seventy mills filled with flour and wheat; have driven in the front of the army over 4,000 head of stock, and have killed and issued to the troops not less than 3,000 sheep." There were tanneries and small ironworks that were destroyed as well.

Sherman believed that the Confederacy derived its strength not from its fighting forces but from the material and moral support of sympathetic Southern whites. Factories, farms and railroads provided Confederate troops with the things they needed, he reasoned, and if he could destroy those things, the Confederate war effort would collapse. Meanwhile, his troops could undermine Southern morale by making life so unpleasant for Georgia's civilians that they would demand an end to the war. Lincoln and Grant did not have a formal policy of taking the war to civilians. They realized that the tactics they were using—engaging in battles and taking prisoners—had no end as long as civilians supported the rebel cause. They would have to take the war to the doorsteps of civilians.

Shortly after Sheridan's maneuvers beginning on November 15, Sherman split his sixty-two-thousand-man army into two wings that marched about thirty miles apart and headed to Savannah. But it was not just Union forces that destroyed supplies. Some Confederate troops went ahead of Sherman and destroyed food stores so that Sherman's troops could not use them because Union troops had to live off the land after they left Atlanta. Sherman arrived in Savannah on December 21, 1864. The city was poorly defended. He presented the city as a Christmas gift to Lincoln along with twenty-five thousand bales of cotton. From there, his army continued on into South and North Carolina in early 1865.

For years after the war ended, a chimney standing in an open field was called a "Sherman," with the implication that Sherman's troops burned down the house that once stood beside the fireplace even in areas Sherman never saw. Richmond's population and the Army of Northern Virginia would feel the effects of this portion of the war directly.

RICHMOND SCARCITIES

By the third year of war, the very fabric of Richmond had begun to fray. Buildings and homes were not repaired due to lack of materials and craftsmen. Although Richmond was never bombarded directly, it could not keep up repairs. Besides the physical aspects of the city, its spirit was frayed and tattered. The euphoria of the first two years of the war had given way under the hammering of inflation and shortages and victories by Union forces.

Emory Thomas wrote, "For three years the city had lived by wit, sacrifice, and will. Now precious little remained to be sacrificed. Richmond discovered that even the most inventive mind could not feed the city when there was no food. Even a genius could not defend the capital without sufficient troops and supplies. As the city realized that no sacrifice within her power would be great enough even her spirits faltered." By the end of 1864, wheat from the Shenandoah Valley used at the Gallego mills in Richmond was no longer available. Alternative supplies from Georgia and the Carolinas could not provide replacements either. Not only had the means of production been destroyed but also stores of food and the railroads to transport them.

However, many believed that the Confederacy could still pull out victories against Grant because Grant had only won because of the overwhelming resources at his disposal in the Western Theater. The Confederate commanders in the Western Theater he faced were not as good as Lee, they argued. But Grant's strategy planned encirclement movements and then to chip away at the perimeter of the rebellion. Additionally, Union troops would drive deep into the South and strike at vital points. This would cut the support and supplies available to the Army of Northern Virginia. They strengthened the blockade in an effort to destroy morale.

The problem boiled down to the growing weakness of the Army of Northern Virginia. The troops had been through a lot. Farmers who enlisted and still served in the army got more and more pleading letters from wives back home who had grown tired of holding on. Desertions rose. According to Joseph Glatthaar, by 1865 desertions were estimated at 120 every day. What soldier would not strongly consider desertion if he received a letter from home that said:

> "We haven't got nothing in the house to eat but a little bit of meal," one woman wrote her soldier husband. "Try to get off and come home and fix us all up some and then you can go back. If you put off coming, t'wont be no use to come, for we'll all…be out there in the garden in the graveyard with your ma and mine."[40]

The very culture that most Southern soldiers came from worked against the military discipline that would have improved the ability of the Army of Northern Virginia to operate. Lastly, casualties decimated the ranks. Glatthaar said that hospitals admitted 102,000 soldiers in May, June and July 1864. For the period from September 1862 through July 1864, Virginia hospitals admitted 413,000 patients. The army could not even find food to steal. To top it all off, by mid-1864 the CSA had lost 1,600 officers, along with 6,000 officers wounded. No army can replace the skill, training and experience of that magnitude without being severely weakened. It only remained for the civilian population of Richmond to understand what was happening.

During the spring and summer of 1864, it became clear that minds in Richmond were almost evenly divided between despair and continued hope for victory. Sallie Brock Putnam extolled the virtue of the Confederacy and its cause, while Varina Davis, the First Lady, began to speculate what actions she would take to protect her family. With purple prose, Sallie Brock Putnam wrote, "Defeat was nowhere written on our future prospects. Discouragement might be, but not defeat nowhere! And we once more hugged to our bosoms the phantom of hope, and it sang a lullaby to our fears, and the Confederate metropolis pursued its usual busy routine, and contented itself with the thought that 'the end is not!'" But on April 1, Mary Chesnut recorded that Varina Davis was "utterly depressed" and believed that the fall of Richmond was not far off. Varina Davis said that she would send her children to Mrs. Chesnut and another friend, Mrs. Preston. Mrs. Davis probably heard more about the rawness of life on the front, while Sallie Brock Putnam saw life in the city but was spared the most gruesome details.

Newspapers and preachers were expected to support the morale of the wider population. On April 8, Reverend Seth Doggett of Centenary Methodist Church preached a sermon that exhorted his congregation to continue to expect victory, that the enemy was factious and nearly insolvent, neither of which was true. Earlier in 1864, former Virginia governor Henry Wise said that slavery was a dead issue, at least in Virginia, regardless of who won the war. At the end, Lee was willing to accept African Americans into the Army of Northern Virginia, and slaves had been working as wage earners in every factory in the city.

SHORTAGES IN 1865…BUT WORSE THIS TIME

Supplies of food normally stored from the previous year were in early spring of 1864 exhausted before farmers could begin to harvest spring plantings. Emory Thomas said, "This year much of the surrounding acreage lay despoiled by fighting, and many farms were in possession of the enemy." This was due to the encircling and encroaching way Union forces moved toward Richmond. Sallie Brock Putnam provided an assessment of the food markets available to private citizens: "Our markets presented a most impoverished aspect. A few stalls at which was sold poor beef, and some at which a few potatoes and other vegetables were placed for sale, were about all that were opened in Richmond markets."

A number of initiatives to address these kinds of issues were put forth. The General Assembly allowed a state warehouse to sell cotton yarn and cotton cards, which were used to pull cotton fibers to a texture that can be converted to yarn at cost. With these basic materials, citizens could make their own cloth and clothes. Salt was unavailable, so the Assembly authorized the governor to impress the mine at Saltville. The Haxall and

Crenshaw flour mills sold flour to make bread at reduced prices to the city's poor. Robert E. Lee turned down an offer for a house from the city, asking instead that the money go to aid families of his troops. The city borrowed money to purchase and distribute food. But the most extraordinary effort to alleviate suffering came from the governor of Virginia, William "Extra Billy" Smith.

Smith planned to buy, transport and resell staple items to people in Richmond. However, the Virginia State Senate rejected the appropriations bill. He turned to expropriating the state's civic and military contingency funds of $40,000 each and borrowed $30,000 from William H. MacFarland's Farmer's Bank. With these funds, he hired a master blockade runner and sent him abroad with cotton to exchange for supplies. This worked for a short time, until the ports of Wilmington and Charleston were seized and the blockade tightened. Smith also commandeered a train from the York River Railroad. He reminded the president of the railroad that the state was his largest shareholder. But by engaging in these enterprises, he put the state in direct competition with private enterprise. He was successful getting the price of rice down to fifty cents per pound and still turning a profit.

Another idea was to lessen the population of the city. The government went so far as to transfer three hundred women whose job was to sign treasury notes to Columbia, South Carolina. It was quickly apparent that measures of this kind did not appreciably reduce the demand for food and impaired the functioning of the government unnecessarily. Prisoner transfer was another matter though. Some prisoners were transferred to Danville, Salisbury and Andersonville. Grant, by ending prisoner exchanges, made the life of Union prisoners worse because the Confederacy could not even feed itself and would never be able to care for the number of prisoners it had.

How Nice It Must Be in Heaven

In his book *Rebel Richmond*, Stephen Ash related the story of Thomas Johnson, who lived in Alexandria and Washington, D.C., until he was sold to a new master in 1853 when he turned seventeen and lived in Richmond until the end of the war. He remembered the sayings of his mother about better times coming and that he could resist his station in life sometimes. His mother told him if he learned to read and write, he might be able to gain his freedom, but if he did, he must keep it a secret. She told him her vision of heaven: "There would be no slaves—all would be free."

Stephen Ash wrote, "Southern whites before and during the Civil War were convinced that slavery and white supremacy were not only necessary for the safety and prosperity of society but also morally beneficent, and they created a vast network of racial laws, institutions, and customs to enforce their will." Public speeches and Sunday sermons supported the racist bias of the white citizens of Richmond. There were dissenters, but the majority believed in the laws, sermons, public speeches and newspaper pronouncements of the need to keep slavery in place and to support their way of life. There is no reason to repeat the vile and morally repugnant statements and beliefs from those times. Suffice it to say that society from top to bottom supported the belief system necessary to keep the war effort going.

The laws and ordinances restricting the movements of African Americans, either slave or free, at the start of the war were a continuation of laws already on the books as well as additional restrictions due the war. The laws had two purposes: one, to prevent an armed uprising and, two, to prevent African Americans from asserting any hint of social equality with whites.

To prevent an uprising like Gabriel's Rebellion in 1800 or Nat Turner's in Southampton County in 1831, African Americans slave or free could not possess a gun, ammunition, a sword or even a Bowie knife on penalty of thirty-nine lashes on a public whipping post. They could not even carry a cane at night or be away from home at night without written passes from their owner or public authority. Freed men and women had to carry registration papers at all times.

To prevent any breach of racial separation and maintain the caste system created by these laws and strictures, even for freed slaves, layers of rules were imposed on African Americans. Freedmen and slaves could not smoke in public, could not possess liquor, had to give way to white people on sidewalks and more. Virginia officially required freed slaves to leave the state after 1806, but many remained in violation of the law. Richmond had 2,576 freedmen—either born free or freed some other way. The bottom line was that African Americans had to get permission from someone white to do almost anything. Even African American churches had to have a white pastor.

Many whites with a conscience and sense of fairness tempered the harshness of the system, but not Mayor Joseph Mayo, who consistently handed down harsh punishments. A prominent merchant, William Brent, who purchased Thomas Johnson, considered his slaves as part of his family.

There are probably many instances of individuals who helped African Americans avoid these very restrictive ordinances and laws. Elizabeth Van Lew, an ardent Unionist and sometimes spy, treated her slaves well. Like with Thomas Jefferson's relationship with Sally Hemings, Silas Omohundro, a prominent slave dealer, had five children with Corinna Hinton. Corinna lived in a house next door to Omohundro, and her light skin made it possible for her to pass as white. At his death in 1864, he granted her and their five children freedom along with a substantial financial gift. Ash wrote, "Although Silas's relationship with Corinna (who had served as his housekeeper) and their children may not have been a secret to his white intimates, the public revelation of it no doubt came as a surprise to other Richmonders."

It can be argued that slavery had been breaking down for decades. Accusations of the abuse of a small child, Josephine, by her owner, Jacob Hoeflick, once came before the authorities. Neighbors testified that he beat the child so hard they could hear the beatings. Alas, by the time he was stopped the child had died. The injustice inflicted on four-year-old Josephine—or "Joe," as she was known—had to cause some of those neighbors to question the institution of slavery.

RICHMOND IN DECLINE—THE LAST YEAR

On the war front, another factor in the final years of the war was that Union armies and commanders improved more than those on the Confederate side. Whatever advantages the Confederacy enjoyed at the start of the war eroded as year after year took their toll. The South's manufacturing capacity simply could not provide replacements for all the shoes, railroad rolling stock and rails, uniforms, armaments and an array of many other necessities required to keep up a war. The South was slow to learn from its mistakes. Frontal assaults should never be undertaken by an army that lacks the ability to replace its manpower. The frontal assault at Gaines's Mill was more devastating than Pickett's Charge at Gettysburg. One would expect that a general order to never engage in a frontal assault against an enemy position would have been in place. Union generals made similar mistakes, but the Confederacy could ill afford it.

Another factor was the way the Confederate government managed its finances. Taxation was rarely used by the South and only slightly more by the North. Bonds were the backbone of finances for both sides, but the

South simply could not borrow what it needed. Even a strategy to sell cotton abroad (if they could get it through the blockade) failed because planters refused to accept Confederate bonds. The Confederate Treasury simply printed money. This inevitably led to rampant inflation. Farmers withheld supplies from the market expecting prices to rise or simply unwilling to take a constantly falling currency in payment. While there were adequate food supplies across the South as a whole, the army and Richmond faced food shortages. Policies proposed by Secretary of the Treasury Christopher G. Memminger and approved by the Confederate Congress harmed the Confederate army and economy.

Chapter 15

THE FALL OF RICHMOND

The winter of 1864–65 was one of the harshest on recent record, and the overcast skies and subfreezing temperatures did nothing to invigorate the struggling population or men in the trenches. Desertion in the lines around Petersburg reached alarming numbers, sometimes hundreds daily. The provost and police in the city could not possibly keep up with all of the transient traffic moving through and in and (mostly) out of the city. The exact population during this time, not known with exactitude, was undoubtedly plummeting from the wartime high of more than 100,000 humans (as many as 125,000 plus counting soldiers on leave, stationed in the city and so on).

By March 1865, the war effort and the economy were in desperate straits, and Richmond, according to Emory Thomas, had begun to metaphorically (and in some cases literally) embody what was left of the Confederate nation. And that nation was dying. There were those who still spoke words of hope and victory, but no one was sure even they believed them. There were also profiteers still trying to make as much money as they could; Robert Lumpkin, slave trader, was still taking orders, sending proxies out and trying to manage his profits wisely as the value of the Confederate dollar plummeted. The next month, as Richmond fell, slaves purchased at the auction on Saturday were quickly sent out of the city. Only fifty slaves—men, women and children— remained at Lumpkin's jail after they were refused space on the last trains out of the city. Lumpkin tried to preserve his "inventory," since they would be of no value to him the next day. Until the last minute, most Southerners believed that their way of life would continue somewhere—additional proof that war would be the only way to bring about this tumultuous change.

Signs of the end were evident inside and out. Mary Chesnut was back in South Carolina, but she still sensed that the end was near on March 30:

> *General Lee says to the men who shirk duty, "This is the people's war; when they tire, I stop."* [Confederate senator Louis] *Wigfall says, "It is all over; the game is up." He is on his way to Texas, and when the hanging begins he can step over into Mexico.*

The geographic integrity of the erstwhile nation had been cut into two and then diced into pieces. There was no longer any regular communication with CSA authorities west of the Mississippi, Tennessee was in Union hands and Sherman had cut the Southeast off and was now marching northward through North Carolina. Grant, of course, surrounded Richmond in his continuing siege, which centered on Petersburg and aimed to cut Richmond's railroad lifelines.

Many reasonable strategists on both sides had realized by early 1865 that Richmond was the target, the war and the cause—the solution to ending the bloodshed. Lincoln perhaps grasped this, even though he was still of the mindset that General U.S. Grant had always had about crushing Lee's army in order to crush the rebellion. What everyone began to realize in early 1865, however, was that Richmond was Lee's army—not only the actual men but also the remaining hospitals, military stores, food, horses, wagons, ships and even a large part of the spirit of the Confederacy itself. Lincoln had refused a peace mission requiring unconditional surrender. T.C. DeLeon wrote in his memoirs, "The tremendous efforts to capture the Capital; the superhuman exertions to defend it in the last four years, had made Richmond the cause." Imagine a huge funnel with Confederate lands and cities in it. Starting with New Orleans and Grant's victories in the Western Theater, on and on with the loss of Vicksburg and the Mississippi River, followed by losses across Tennessee, the taking of Mobile Bay and Sherman taking Atlanta, Savannah and Charleston. All these names falling like sand out of an hourglass. Closer to Richmond, Sheridan laid waste the Shenandoah Valley, and Grant surrounded Petersburg and Richmond. The capital would be the last piece, ending with Lee's surrender at Appomattox Court House as the last grain to fall.

In March 1865, public services continued to break down: gas lines needed repair, garbage of all types had accumulated, looting was increasing as police and provost officials joined desperate city defense forces, businesses were closing and mail service was erratic.

BACKGROUND TO THE FALL OF RICHMOND

On the early morning of April 2, 1865, General Horatio Wright formed his more than 14,000 men into a wedge formation that charged the Confederate line at Petersburg, manned by only 2,800 soldiers. The attack plunged through abatis (sharpened tree trunks or limbs pointed toward the enemy) and over the breastworks. Here, at the end of nearly ten months, the Union finally broke through the main Confederate line. This was the last attack. Lee telegraphed the War Department that he intended to evacuate Petersburg and Richmond that night. The Union occupied both Petersburg and Richmond the next day.

On Sunday, April 2, 1865, while attending St. Paul's Church, President Jefferson Davis received from the War Department the report from General Lee that his lines had been breached and that the citadel would finally fall. Most high-ranking officials, including Davis, had already sent their children, wives and families to safer areas. Those who were left were the poor, in the military or government or still trying at the last minute to make a profit.

Although there were plans to destroy factories, warehouses and military stores, there would be no time to evacuate everything in the case of the city falling—those plans were not fully communicated as of April 2—nor would they be exercised, according to a complete plan:

> *Sunday, April 2, 1865, came to be known as Evacuation Sunday. The note from Lee read in part, "I see no prospect of doing more than holding our position here till night. I am not certain that I can do that....I advise that all preparation be made for leaving Richmond to-night." Jefferson Davis had expected that Lee could provide several days' warning. How could the Confederate government or any government adequately pack up in one day and leave town? Davis called a Cabinet meeting in the former Custom House at the base of Capitol Square, inviting Governor Smith and Mayor Mayo. He relayed Lee's message and ordered an evacuation for that night. Confederate General Ewell received orders to leave with his troops numbering only about 5,000 after dark.*[41]

While there had been no initial panic, it did not take long for chaos to foment. The Treasury Department boxed gold and silver but had to burn some paper money and records. When the War Department filled two boxcars for Danville and had no more room, it, too, burned the records that were left in the streets. Prisoners were still being escorted to Libby and other prisons, even as frantic efforts were made to move Union prisoners out of town at the same time. Slaves were still being bought and sold. The mayor met with the city council in the afternoon to discuss how to handle the inevitable thirst that would manifest soon for the great stores of liquor still in the city—importantly, however, they did not discuss a detailed plan for how to surrender the city.

Word traveled quickly, and soon there was a palpable buzz, anxiety and tension in the air. James Hawkins, who worked for the Southern Express Company and who had already seen one cache of government "coin" safely delivered to the city of Charlotte, North Carolina, was back in Richmond on the second and would end up evacuating more CSA money and documents. He recorded some of what he saw:

> *Found everything in an awful excited condition burning valuable paper and money at all the different Departs—Treasury, War, Medical, State Capitol of Va etc.—destroying all that they supposed would be of any service to U.S. Govt. Found they had also pressed the Company's horses etc. but they were after liberated by orders "Secty of War." I went to Central Depot supposing I might find some of the boys going Home & send a letter to you all, but no chance.*[42]

Hawkins and his colleagues, like the military, split their loads up—Hawkins left around midnight by roads north of the James and his colleagues by roads south of the river. This meant that some of the cargo would hopefully make it through to Lynchburg or Danville. If one group was captured, the other might make it through.

Under orders from Confederate general Richard S. Ewell, the fleeing Confederates added to the confusion in their haste to evacuate. Here two soldiers guarded a train and stayed on duty; there police and soldiers turned away as looting began. A mob formed once people began to realize what was happening. General Ewell was commander of the Richmond Military District garrison, having been reassigned there after Lee ignominiously had to take over Ewell's men during the Battle of Spotsylvania Court House when he was ineffective. Ewell was generally talented and capable but was also haunted by his perceived failure at Gettysburg to take the high ground. In Richmond, he oversaw much of the evacuation and, ironically, was now giving up the high ground.

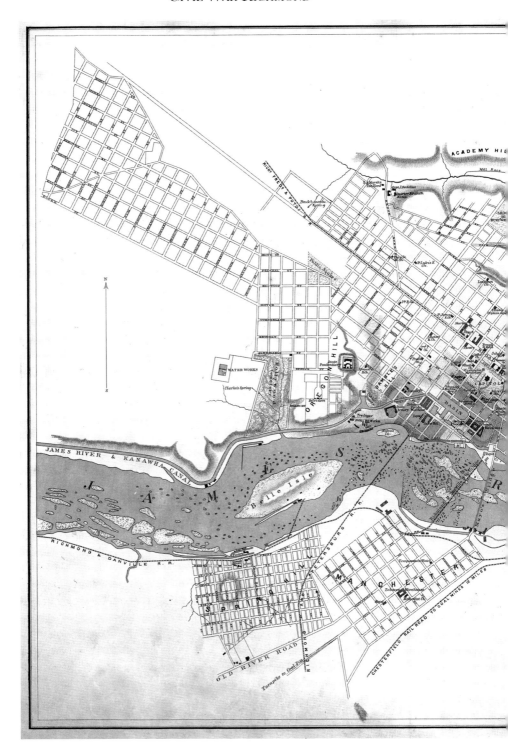

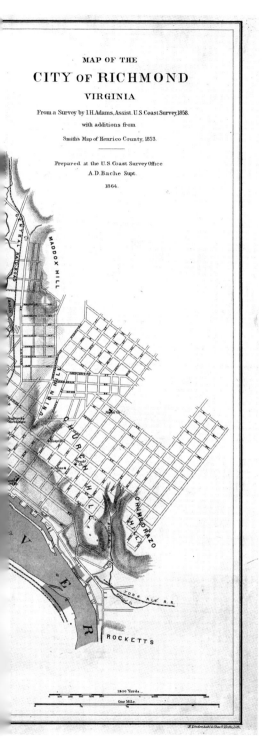

Map of Richmond with burned districts.
Library of Congress.

People were coming into Richmond almost as rapidly as they were leaving:

In the midst of the chaos, the wife and children of General A.P. Hill, who had been killed earlier on Sunday, rode in a wagon with his body back to Richmond anticipating burial in Hollywood Cemetery. When the wagon reached the south end of the bridge, it had to wait until after midnight, long enough for the torrent of south-bound traffic to abate. They took the body to a building on Capitol Square and then set out to find a pine casket. They went to Belvin's furniture store and, when no one answered, went in anyway. They found an undersized box and struggled to get the body in. There was now no way to get to Hollywood Cemetery, so they turned around and headed to the family home back across the bridge, but this time going with the flow of traffic south. His remains were reinterred in 1891 at the intersection of Laburnum and Hermitage Road in a monument paid for by Lewis Ginter.[43]

In the afternoon, facts began to coalesce. The last railroad line south had been broken, the lines at Petersburg had been breached and the city militia was ordered to the fortifications to relieve regulars so they could head south to the focal point. Peter Helms Mayo, twenty-nine-year-old officer assigned to the Department of Transportation, received word to organize two trains to carry gold bullion and government records to Danville. Railroad workers scrambled at the terminal to put together the required cars and engines:

Libby Prison was evacuated, and prisoners departed on a flag-of-truce boat that had been sent with supplies collected from northern charities. Everyone that day, whether prisoner, slave, soldier, citizen, upper-class, working class, Confederate, Unionist, burglar or freedman, was heading somewhere. The state penitentiary held no prisoners either after a few prisoners got out of their cells and forced the guards to give them keys to the other cells. About 300 inmates took to the streets.[44]

Outside the city, Union general Godfrey Weitzel knew that the Confederate lines had been broken but was overly cautious, worrying that there were inner defenses remaining yet beyond the outer ones now severed. Perhaps he could have judged from the noise and smoke that the city was digressing into a chaos that could only happen with military abandonment, but he erred on the side of caution. Using field glasses, his men counted thirty-eight rail cars heading south with troops on them. Even then, he still hesitated. Fires could be seen breaking out. It would be the middle of night before he sent men

Above: Chapin's Farm, Virginia. General Godfrey Weitzel's headquarters and band of the Eighteenth Corps. *Library of Congress.*

Right: General Godfrey Weitzel. *Library of Congress.*

forward, and they found empty fortifications. He wired U.S. Grant that he would head into the city in the morning.

The mayor's plan for controlling liquor—giving chits to businesses for credit and then destroying their stocks with axes—did not work. In fact, it may in some cases have actually opened the doors for the growing mobs who roamed, sometimes with cups in hand, from place to place looting and drinking more. The streets were filled with an otherworldly mix of deserters, free and enslaved African Americans, POWs, paupers, government officials and endless refugees.

The Richmond *Whig* reported on April 6, 1865, an escape during the evacuation that shows the chaos of that night:

> *Captain Sidney S. Grovnor, of the United States Secret Service, and John Hancock, both lately held as prisoners in Castle Thunder by the Confederate authorities, upon the charge of being Union spies. In the height of the evacuation they were brought out with other prisoners to be marched off, but on their way through the city their guard stopped to drink some whisky running in the gutters, its destruction then going on. This opportunity the captives embraced to escape, and they remained concealed until the advance of the Union forces entered the city. Hancock was confined in a dungeon, and his life was in jeopardy.*

After darkness, the pace picked up inside the city as people worked by moonlight. Word had spread further, and the steady stream of refugees was moving through the streets even late at night. In addition to the moonlight, the many growing fires were providing an ethereal glow, with long shadows falling across the streets and alleyways. The fires intentionally started at warehouses and military facilities by Ewell's men were now spreading to other parts of the central city. Hawkins's company headquarters was soon in ruins, along with countless packages and letters that hadn't made it into the wagons. When the city magazine exploded in the early morning, eight people were killed in the neighboring poorhouse. VMI cadets who would have also been in the path of the blast had just left for the front a while earlier. The chaos and destruction would become fully evident in the smoky haze of morning on April 3.

Around 3:00 a.m., naval officials scuttled the James River Fleet, and there were more fires and explosions to accompany those being started by Ewell's men on land. The unfinished ironclad gunboat CSS *Texas* somehow escaped the destruction, along with a small gunboat, but everything else in the fleet was burned, scuttled or sunk in the river. It represented a collective loss of tens of thousands of dollars of precious iron, machining and thousands of man-hours of labor, destroyed without ever engaging in a major fight (although some argue that the fleet's mere existence had an influence).

When Ewell gave the order to torch the warehouses and bridges over the river, the fates seem to respond by whipping up a strong breeze. Some of the roofs contained semi-flammable bituminous material, and the effect was like "Greek fire," with bits of burning paper floating from one roof to another. A conflagration started that made the earlier burnings seem like campfires.

Later, when the city was in Union hands, Richmonders would finally begin to take full stock of the destruction. The *New York Times*, on April 8, soon reported on the spectacle:

> *At present we cannot do more than enumerate some of the most prominent buildings destroyed. These include the Bank of Richmond, Traders' Bank, Bank of the Commonwealth, Bank of Virginia, Farmers' Bank, all the banking houses, the American Hotel, the Columbian Hotel, the Enquirer building on Twelfth-street, the Dispatch Office and job rooms, corner of*

Burning and evacuation of Richmond, April 3, 1865. *Currier & Ives Engraving, Library of Congress.*

Custom house (*left*) and capitol after the evacuation fire. *Library of Congress.*

> *Thirteenth and Main streets; all that block of buildings known as Devlin's Block; the Examiner Office, engine and machinery rooms; the Confederate Post-office Department building; the State Court-house; a fine old building situated on Capitol-square, at its Franklin-street entrance; the Mechanics' Institute, vacated by the Confederate States War Department, and all the buildings on that square up to Eighth-street and back to Main-street; the confederate arsenal and laboratory, Seventh-street.*

Ultimately, the devastation spoke to the hopelessness of the Southern cause. The fall of Richmond felt like the end of everything. A correspondent for a Northern paper captured it this way:

Ruins of Gallego mills. *Library of Congress.*

But as I entered the burned district, no more, even of these, were encountered. All was solitude. The moon gave a picturesque and the sullen lames a weird and supernatural light to the scene. As far as the eye could reach in every direction were only ruins, irregular piles of brick, thin fragments of walls yet standing, sometimes a single chimney of pillar alone remaining upright of a large block—and even as I looked, perhaps one of these would topple over into the street, already piled thickly with fallen bricks.[45]

THE SURRENDER OF RICHMOND

The next morning, even as the fires continued to burn, Mayor Mayo and a few members of the city council set out to find a commanding Union authority to offer up surrender of the city. With no white flag immediately at hand, they reportedly tore parts of their shirts off to create a makeshift white flag. At the same time, General Weitzel's men were entering the outskirts of the city. A meeting soon took place, and Richmond officially ceased to be the capital of the Confederate States of America.

The *New York Times* on April 8 reported on the events:

> *After the surrender of the city, and its occupation by Gen. Weitzel, about 10 o'clock, vigorous efforts were set on foot to stop the progress of the flames. The soldiers reinforced the fire brigade, and labored nobly, and with great success. The flames east on Main-street, were checked by the blowing up of the Traders' Bank about noon. The flames gradually died out at various points as material failed for them to feed upon; but in particular localities the work of destruction went on until towards 3 or four o'clock, when the mastery of the flames was obtained, and Richmond was safe from utter desolation.*

It was a stunning scene for anyone who had been in Richmond before and after the surrender. There are many accounts of citizens walking around somewhat aimlessly, apparently (and understandably) in shock. The arriving Union soldiers began helping put the fires out; sometimes crowds of newly freed slaves and children followed them around. Because the mobs had destroyed hoses and other firefighting infrastructure, fire breaks were built, including demolished buildings. Although the granite custom house and the capitol building had escaped, roughly nine hundred other buildings in the center of the business district were in ruins, including the ten-story-high ruins of Gallego mills. Weitzel's troops began to share food and generally behaved in ways that began to reassure people that the new occupation would not begin with more violence.

"The pavements are filled with pulverized glass," Confederate War Department clerk John Jones wrote in his diary. "My diary is surely drawing to a close."

People reacted in various ways to the abrupt change in status:

> *Confederate loyalists became bitter and dispirited. Formerly enslaved people were ecstatic at the fall of the city and Unionists finally could express their true feelings. Union troops were greeted by flags being displayed that had been hidden for many years. Union troops sent to protect Elizabeth Van Lew from vengeful Confederates found a large Union flag flying from the roof of her Church Hill home and had no doubt which house they were to protect.*[46]

Above: Custom house, still standing after the evacuation fire. *Library of Congress.*

Left: Plaque, Tenth and Main. *Photo by Derek Kannemeyer.*

Above: Ruins of Exchange Bank, Main Street, April, 1865. *Library of Congress.*

Opposite: Federal courthouse today on Main Street. *Photo by Derek Kannemeyer.*

A unique moment in the war occurred when African American Union soldiers marched to Capitol Square, cheered along the way by many of Richmond's thousands of freed African Americans and recently liberated slaves. Truly, the capitalist slave regime was dead in one important sense at this moment.

Before long, the Stars and Stripes rose up over the capitol building. There has been a sizable lore and history around who first raised that flag. One account has Richard G. Forrester, a seventeen-year-old mixed-race grandson of Gustavus Myers (a Jewish lawyer, state legislator and defender of many enslaved persons before Mayor Mayo's court), pulling an American flag out

of hiding he had rescued from the capitol at the beginning of the secession crisis in 1861. A Union officer, Lieutenant Royal Prescott, reportedly had it lowered and took the flag. The *New York Times* later reported that it was Lieutenant Johnston de Peyster and Lieutenant Loomis Langdon of the same Twelfth Maine Volunteers who hoisted another large Union flag with a rich provenance (including flying previously in New Orleans) that officially marked the finality of the transition and the symbolic restoration of federal authority. Lee would surrender at Appomattox six days later, but this marked the end of the war in Richmond.

LINCOLN VISITS RICHMOND

One day later, President Abraham Lincoln, accompanied by his son Tad, walked up the hill from Rockett's Landing toward Capitol Square; he also wanted to see the White House of the Confederacy, where his counterpart had organized four years of war. Lincoln, fifty-six years of age, was escorted only by a few sailors from the ship in which he arrived. The streets even by this time under Union occupation were still filled with drunks, deserters and other shady characters, making Lincoln's "walk" seem risky in hindsight. The risk was more than offset, however, by the joy, admiration and fascination a growing crowd of freed slaves and other African Americans following him expressed openly. Later that day, the

Lincoln on the streets of Richmond, April 4, 1865. *National Portrait Gallery.*

Abe Lincoln and Tad. *American Civil War Museum, photo by Derek Kannemeyer.*

president rode around Richmond in an open carriage, escorted by African American cavalrymen. He seemed fearless. Lincoln by these actions must surely have been full of hope that he could peacefully reunite the nation again, modeling moderation, hope and reconciliation.

Although Lincoln gave a speech at Capitol Square, his words are lost to history. It surely must have included important words for both sides in the conflict. Admiral Porter recollected some of it: "[You can] cast off the name of slave and trample upon it....Liberty is your birthright. God gave it to you as he gave it to others, and it is a sin that you have been deprived of it for so many years." For safety purposes, Lincoln was advised to spend the night back on the ship. Although he would leave the next day to return to Washington, his visit became engrained in the lore of the end of the war.

EPILOGUE

There are myriad consequences left over from Civil War battles and administrative decisions than could ever be dealt with over several volumes. We will endeavor to draw a few conclusions that can be drawn from the experiences of Richmond. Residents of the South, and especially Richmond, were worn down mentally, psychologically, sociologically and financially by the war. Every Richmonder, every year, had less. They weighed less from hunger and lack of proper nutrition. They lost their dignity from lawlessness, prostitution and gambling that spread over the city. What money they still had bought less due to rampant inflation as the war wore on. Almost everyone lost loved ones. Others came to Richmond to retrieve bodies, while soldiers in combat may have lost limbs to the incessant conflict. But they endured similar to the way German citizens did through World War II or other peoples in long conflicts. Within any segment of the population, the degree of suffering varied. During 1865, soldiers from Petersburg to Richmond deserted to Union lines, as did slaves if they could.

Although Washington, D.C., was partially burned and temporarily occupied by the British in 1814 during the War of 1812, no other large American city has suffered the almost utter destruction and long-term occupation by an enemy such as Richmond experienced. Depending on the perspective one takes, this is a dubious, humbling, distressing and thought-provoking exceptionalism for any American city.

Pearl Harbor was smashed by the Japanese air force in 1941; New York was devastated by 9/11; smaller cities like Chambersburg, Pennsylvania, or

Columbia, South Carolina, were burned during the Civil War. A number of cities, including Richmond, suffered during the Revolutionary War. But no city of the relative importance of Richmond has ever been laid under siege for months, later burned and mostly destroyed and then indefinitely occupied by a hostile enemy armed force. Especially in this case, as the occupation was by the very government forces of the nation to which the city (and state of Virginia) belonged to and pledged allegiance to merely four years earlier.

These events, and the long aftermath of the war, make Richmond an anomaly. There isn't really another city to which it can be compared. The other great cities of the antebellum South—and the short-lived Confederate States of America—did not hold the significance or were not throttled in smothering and complete psychological defeat the way Richmond was. New Orleans fell to Union forces early; Atlanta was important but in no way comparable to the importance of Richmond in terms of the military and governmental infrastructure of the CSA, not to the mention its psychological importance as capital; Nashville fell early; Wilmington, Norfolk, Charleston, Mobile, Galveston and other port cities were not the size of Richmond and, due to the Union blockade, were limited in their potential strategic import; and St. Louis, Louisville and Lexington never fell officially into the formalized Confederate sphere of influence. Only Vicksburg, Mississippi, which did not celebrate Independence Day for eighty-one years from 1863, possibly equals Richmond in the devastation and psychological impact from the war.

This left Richmond as the crown jewel, the outlier and ultimately as the sacrificial offering necessary to end the long war. Lee's ragged army lasted in the field for quite some time until the citadel of Richmond fell. Lee's army, along with Johnston's and others, surrendered after the hope of Richmond had been dashed beyond repair.

Richmond today is a medium-size American city and still the important capital city of the state of Virginia. It still utilizes its deep-water port and serves as a financial and industrial center and an important medical and educational mecca. In other ways, though, it is overshadowed by larger cities on the East Coast like Baltimore and Philadelphia, and even of southern cities that have long since recovered from the nineteenth-century fratricidal conflict, Atlanta, Raleigh, Columbia and Birmingham are only a few examples of southern urban revitalization.

Few cities have the historical stretch and girth of Richmond. The Civil War is just one of its chapters, but it was the darkest and overlays much of the city's history since 1865. Bruce Catton best summed up what the war meant everywhere:

> *In the 1860s the leaders of the cotton belt made one of the most prodigious miscalculations in recorded history. On the eve of the era of applied technologies, in which more and more work is done with fewer people and less effort, they made war to preserve the day of chattel slavery—the era of gang labor, with its reliance on the same use of human muscles that built the pyramids. The lost cause was lost before it started to fight. Inability to see what is going on in the world can be costly.*[47]

Tread lightly along the streets in the old parts of Richmond. Someone far different from you, who may have done terrible things, walked there yesterday.

NOTES

Chapter 1

1. Antebellum Richmond, www.antebellumrichmond.com.

Chapter 2

2. Richmond *Dispatch*, April 26, 1862, 2.
3. From Collection Overview of the Heslip-Ruffin Family Papers, 1822–1946, accessed at http://amistadresearchcenter.tulane.edu.
4. Trammell, "Slave Trade in Central Virginia."

Chapter 3

5. Arnold, *History of the Tobacco Industry in Virginia*, 58–59.
6. Coski, *Capital Navy*, 13.

Chapter 7

7. Pond, "Kilpatrick's and Dahlgren's Raid to Richmond," 4:95–96.
8. From the Richmond *Whig*, November 14, 1862, 2.

Chapter 8

9. Virginia Division of Geology and Mineral Resources, "Virginia's Mineral Resources."
10. New Georgia Encyclopedia, "Civil War Industry and Manufacturing."
11. See Dew, *Ironmaker to the Confederacy*; Brady, "Charcoal Iron Industry in Virginia."
12. Richmond *Dispatch*, July 16, 1863.

Chapter 9

13. Eyewitness to History, "Battlefield Tragedy, 1862."
14. McLaws, letter, LM to Emily, October 14, 1863, in *Soldier's General*, 206–7.

Chapter 10

15. Wall, Rogers and Kutney-Lee, "North vs. the South," 37–55.

Chapter 12

16. Illinois University Library, "American Newspapers."
17. Civil War Richmond, "Confederate States Medical and Surgical Journal."
18. Encyclopedia Virginia, "Confederate Newspapers in Virginia."
19. Ash, *Rebel Richmond*, 90.
20. Richmond *Dispatch*, August 18, 1864, 1.

Chapter 13

21. Hacker, Hilde and Jones, "Effect of the Civil War," 39–70.
22. Richmond *Dispatch*, November 26, 1862, 2.
23. Richmond *Dispatch*, June 20, 1861, 1.
24. Richmond *Dispatch*, October 25, 1861, 2.
25. Richmond *Dispatch*, July 28, 1862, 1.

26. Richmond *Dispatch*, May 19, 1863, 1.

27. Richmond *Dispatch*, December 4, 1862, 1.

28. Haines, "Fertility and Mortality in the United States."

29. *New York Tribune*, April 10, 1865, 1.

30. Various wartime newspaper accounts.

31. Various wartime newspaper accounts.

32. Ash, *Rebel Richmond*, 205–7

33. Various wartime newspaper accounts.

34. Richmond *Dispatch*, August 6, 1862.

35. Richmond *Dispatch*, March 28, 1862, 2.

36. Richmond *Dispatch*, January 15, 1863, 2.

37. Richmond *Dispatch*, February 6, 1863, 1.

38. Richmond *Dispatch*, April 25, 1863, 1.

39. Richmond *Dispatch*, July 4, 1862, 2.

Chapter 14

40. Glatthaar, "Why the Confederacy Lost."

Chapter 15

41. Trammell and Terrell, *Short History of Richmond*, 73.

42. Holcomb, "Eyewitness Account of the Evacuation of Richmond."

43. Trammell and Terrell, *Short History of Richmond*, 74.

44. Ibid.

45. *Boston Daily Advertiser*, April 10, 1865, 1.

46. Trammell and Terrell, *Short History of Richmond*, 78.

Epilogue

47. Catton, *Waiting for the Morning Train*.

Bibliography

Arnold, B.W., Jr. *The History of the Tobacco Industry in Virginia from 1860 to 1894.* Baltimore, MD: Johns Hopkins University Press, 1897.

Ash, Stephen V. *Rebel Richmond: Life and Death in the Confederate Capital.* Chapel Hill: University of North Carolina Press, 2019.

Blair, William. *Virginia's Private War: Feeding Body and Soul in the Confederacy: 1861–1865.* Columbia: University of South Carolina Press, 1998.

Brady, T.T. "The Charcoal Iron Industry in Virginia." *Virginia Minerals* 37, no. 4 (1991).

Bridges, P. "John M. Daniel (1825–1865)." Encyclopedia Virginia, 2018. http://www.encyclopediavirginia.org.

Calcutt, Rebecca. *Richmond's Wartime Hospitals.* Gretna, LA: Pelican Publishing, 2005.

Catton, Bruce. *Waiting for the Morning Train: An American Boyhood.* New York City: Doubleday, 1972.

Chesson, Michael B. "Harlots or Heroines? A New Look at the Richmond Bread Riot." *Virginia Magazine of History and Biography* 92, no. 2 (1984): 131–75.

Civil War Richmond. "Confederate States Medical and Surgical Journal." https://civilwarrichmond.com.

Coski, John M. *Capital Navy.* New York: Savas Beatie, 2005.

Dabney, Virginius. *Richmond: The Story of a City.* Charlottesville: University of Virginia Press, 1991.

Dew, Charles B. *Ironmaker to the Confederacy: Joseph R. Anderson and the Tredegar Iron Works.* New Haven, CT: Yale University Press, 1966.

Donald, David Herbert, ed. *Why the North Won the Civil War*. Baton Rouge: Louisiana State University Press, 1960.

Encyclopedia Virginia. "Confederate Newspapers in Virginia during the Civil War." https://www.encyclopediavirginia.org.

Eyewitness to History. "Battlefield Tragedy, 1862." http://www.eyewitnesstohistory.com.

Ferguson, Ernest B. *Ashes of Glory: Richmond at War*. New York: Vintage, 1997.

Glatthaar, Joseph. "Why the Confederacy Lost: The Experiences of Robert E. Lee's Army of Northern Virginia." Talk given on February 8, 2011. https://www.youtube.com/watch?v=Zy3OWWWARvw.

Hacker, J., L. Hilde and J. Jones. "The Effect of the Civil War on Southern Marriage Patterns." *Journal of Southern History* 76, no. 1 (2010): 39–70. JSTOR.

Haines, M. "Fertility and Mortality in the United States." EH.net, 2008. https://eh.net.

Hoehling, A.A. *The Day Richmond Died*. N.p.: Madison Books, 1991.

Holcomb, Julia. "An Eyewitness Account of the Evacuation of Richmond During the American Civil War." HistoryNet, 2003. https://www.historynet.com.

Illinois University Library. "American Newspapers, 1800–1860: An Introduction." https://www.library.illinois.edu.

Lankford, Nelson. *Richmond Burning: The Last Days of the Confederate Capital*. London: Penguin Books, 2003.

McLaws, Lafayette. Letter, LM to Emily, October 14, 1863, camp near Chattanooga, Tennessee. ASG-LM, "Major General Lafayette McLaws," A Soldier's General, site by John Oeffinger. http://asoldiersgeneral.com.

Moore, Samuel J.T. *Moore's Complete Civil War Guide to Richmond*. N.p.: privately published, 1978.

New Georgia Encyclopedia. "Civil War Industry and Manufacturing." https://www.georgiaencyclopedia.org.

Pond, George E. "Kilpatrick's and Dahlgren's Raid to Richmond." In *Battles & Leaders of the Civil War*. Vol. 4 N.p.: Thomas Yoseloff Incorporated, 1956.

Robertson, James I. *Stonewall Jackson: The Man, The Soldier, The Legend*. New York: Macmillan Publishing Company, 1997.

Sears, Stephen W. *To the Gates of Richmond: The Peninsula Campaign*. Boston: Tickner & Fields, 1992.

Thomas, Emory M. *The Confederate State of Richmond: A Biography of the Capital*. Baton Rouge: Louisiana State University Press, 1998.

Thomas, William G. *The Iron Way: Railroads, the Civil War, and the Making of Modern America.* New Haven, CT: Yale University Press, 2011.

Tindall, George Brown, and David Emory Shi. *America: A Narrative History.* New York: W.W. Norton, 1984.

Trammell, J. "Richmond Slave Market Busy to End." *Washington Times,* February 12, 2005.

————. "Richmond's Belle Isle Is Rival to Andersonville." *Washington Times,* August 31, 2002.

————. "The Slave Trade in Central Virginia." Talk given on March 1, 2020, sponsored by the Fluvanna Historical Society, One Shared Story and the Charlottesville Area Community Foundation.

————. "Virginia Railroads Vital to the Southern Cause." *Washington Times,* August 11, 2001.

Trammell, J., and G. Terrell. *A Short History of Richmond.* Charleston, SC: The History Press, 2018.

Virginia Division of Geology and Mineral Resources. "Virginia's Mineral Resources and the Civil War." https://www.dmme.virginia.gov.

Wall, B., K. Rogers and A. Kutney-Lee. "The North vs. the South: Conditions at Civil War Hospitals." *Southern Quarterly* 53, no. 3–4 (Spring/Summer 2016): 37–55.

Wixson, Neal E., ed. *From Civility to Survival: Richmond Ladies during the Civil War: The Ladies Reveal Their Wartime Private Thoughts and Struggles in Compelling Diaries and Emotional Memories.* N.p.: iUniverse, 2012.

WEB SOURCES

americanantiquarian.org
asoldiersgeneral.com
biography.com
civilwarrichmond.com
dmme.virginia.gov
eh.net
encyclopediavirginia.org
eyewitnesstohistory.com
georgiaencyclopedia.org
historynet.com
library.illinois.edu

INDEX

cotton 21, 22, 49, 53, 79, 94, 96,
    97, 98, 163, 165, 166, 169,
    191

D

Dahlgren affair 68
Daniel, John Moncure 133, 134,
    135
Daughters of Charity 110
Davis, Jefferson 55, 68, 83, 84, 85,
    93, 94, 95, 96, 97, 100, 123,
    133, 134, 140, 142, 146, 148,
    172
Davis, Varina 94, 146, 148, 164
Dickens, Charles 16, 17
Drewry's Bluff 67, 73, 84, 158

E

Ewell, Richard S., General 172,
    173, 178, 179

F

First Battle of Bull Run 68, 101,
    103, 122
Ford, Robert 128
Fort Sumter 53, 76, 120

G

Gallego 37, 76, 163, 182
Germans 18, 47, 189
Gorgas, Josiah 98

Grant, Ulysses S., General 42, 45,
    60, 88, 119, 157, 158, 159,
    160, 161, 162, 164, 166, 171,
    176
"Great Escape, the" (Libby Prison)
    128

H

Halleck, Henry W., General 42, 159
haunted sites 66
Hemings, Sally 168
Henry, Patrick 15, 23
Hill, Ambrose Powell, Jr., General
    87, 89, 91, 176
Hoge, Moses D., Reverend 55, 64
Hollywood Cemetery 66, 134, 148,
    149, 154, 176

I

ironclads 67, 76, 78, 82

J

Jackson, Mary 140, 141, 142
Jackson, Thomas J. "Stonewall" 84,
    87, 89, 91, 96, 154
James River 15, 16, 19, 32, 36, 39,
    73, 76, 78, 84, 85, 112, 116,
    159, 162, 178
Jefferson, Thomas 15, 168
Jews 38, 48, 184
Johnson, Thomas 26, 166, 167
Johnston, Joseph E., General 83,
    84, 85, 190

About the Authors

GUY TERRELL coauthored *A Short History of Richmond* (also from The History Press) and *The Fourth Branch of Government: We the People* with Jack Trammell. He has also published poems in *Tar River Poetry Review* and *Streetlight*. He earned his BA at Hampden-Sydney College, an MBA from George Mason University and an MS in information systems from Virginia Commonwealth University. He is a past president and treasurer of the Poetry Society of Virginia.

JACK TRAMMELL is author of more than twenty books, including *The Richmond Slave Trade*. He teaches at Mount Saint Mary's University in Maryland, where he specializes in social history and disability history. He can be reached at jacktrammell@yahoo.com.